DIVIDEND INVESTING

DIVIDEND INVESTING

Dependable Income to Navigate
All Market Environments

**JENNY VAN LEEUWEN
HARRINGTON**

HARRIMAN HOUSE LTD
3 Viceroy Court
Bedford Road
Petersfield
Hampshire
GU32 3LJ
GREAT BRITAIN
Tel: +44 (0)1730 233870

Email: enquiries@harriman-house.com
Website: harriman.house

First published in 2025.

Copyright © Jenny Van Leeuwen Harrington

The right of Jenny Van Leeuwen Harrington to be identified as the Author has been asserted in accordance with the Copyright, Design and Patents Act 1988.

Paperback ISBN: 978-1-80409-046-6
eBook ISBN: 978-1-80409-047-3

British Library Cataloguing in Publication Data
A CIP catalogue record for this book can be obtained from the British Library.

All rights reserved; no part of this publication may be reproduced, stored in a retrieval system, or transmitted in any form or by any means, electronic, mechanical, photocopying, recording, or otherwise without the prior written permission of the Publisher. This book may not be lent, resold, hired out or otherwise disposed of by way of trade in any form of binding or cover other than that in which it is published without the prior written consent of the Publisher.

Whilst every effort has been made to ensure that information in this book is accurate, no liability can be accepted for any loss incurred in any way whatsoever by any person relying solely on the information contained herein.

No responsibility for loss occasioned to any person or corporate body acting or refraining to act as a result of reading material in this book can be accepted by the Publisher, by the Author, or by the employers of the Author.

The Publisher does not have any control over or any responsibility for any Author's or third-party websites referred to in or on this book.

This book is dedicated to my incredible clients, past and present. Through your years and decades of support, patience and confidence in me, more than any text book or business school class ever could have, you have taught me how to become a great investor. I am forever grateful.

ABOUT THE AUTHOR

Jenny Van Leeuwen Harrington is the chief executive officer of Gilman Hill Asset Management, LLC, an income-focused, boutique investment management firm located in New Canaan, CT. She also serves as portfolio manager of the firm's flagship equity income strategy, which she created and has managed since its inception. In this capacity, she is responsible for an equity portfolio with a mandate of generating a 5% or higher aggregate annual dividend yield, with additional potential for capital appreciation.

Prior to joining Gilman Hill in 2006, Jenny was a vice president in private wealth management at Neuberger Berman. She began her Wall Street career as an analyst in Goldman Sachs' private client services group of the equities division, and later became an associate in the investment management division. Jenny has served over the years on many investment committees that have ranged from university endowments to large family offices. She also serves on the board of directors for the Council for Economic Education and Sibley Memorial Hospital, where she is additionally vice chair of the investment committee.

A sought-after expert on dividend investing, Jenny is regularly quoted in major business publications such as *The Wall Street Journal* and *Barron's*. She is a regular commentator on CNBC's *The Halftime Report*.

CONTENTS

PREFACE 1

FOREWORD 3

INTRODUCTION 7

Part 1: Theory of Dividend Investing

1. What is a Dividend? 19
2. Emotional Comfort 31
3. What Types of Companies Choose to Pay Dividends and Why? 43

Part 2: The Practice of Dividend Investing

4. Screening 61
5. Researching Dividend Companies 69
6. Structuring a Dividend Stock Portfolio 95
7. Managing Dividend Cuts and Reductions 105
8. Sell Discipline 113

Part 3: Case Studies of People and Stocks

9. Bill and His Demand for Income, Income, Income!   *127*
10. National Properties Trust   *137*
11. Carol Told Her Broker, "I Cannot Lose Money!"   *145*
12. H&R Block   *153*
13. Larry and Lori and the Outer Banks Rental Property   *161*
14. Enterprise Products Partners L.P.   *169*
15. The Sherris   *177*
16. Advance Auto Parts   *185*
17. Henry versus MaryAnne   *193*
18. Short Tales of Many Woes and Value Traps—New York Community Bank, Lumen and Cherokee   *203*
19. Doctor Kemp   *211*

CONCLUDING THOUGHTS   217

EPILOGUE   221

A NOTE ON THE COVER   225

ACKNOWLEDGMENTS   227

PREFACE

WHAT THIS BOOK IS ABOUT

THIS is a book about investing in dividend income-oriented stocks, building actively managed dividend income stock portfolios and all of the associated pragmatic and emotional benefits related to this style of investing. It does not focus on dividend income fund selection or evaluation. It also does not focus on the use of derivatives or leverage to enhance investment portfolio income.

WHO THIS BOOK IS FOR

While told through the lens of dividend investing, the book serves as a how-to manual for being a thoughtful, disciplined investor. It helps investors think about portfolio utility and the importance of emotional control in long-term investment success. The step-by-step process and storytelling serve as a guide to creating a sound research process, a robust sell discipline and a framework to determine portfolio structure and position sizing.

HOW THIS BOOK IS STRUCTURED

Readers will enjoy a practical, replicable how-to manual, followed by illustrative real-life case studies showcasing both client situations and successful and unsuccessful investments.

FOREWORD BY CHARLES D. ELLIS

We all know—or certainly should know—that the key to long-term investing success is to have a plan we can and will stick with that's right for each of us. Since we are all unique in investment skills, interest in and time for investing, wealth, age, responsibilities, and a host of other variables, we should each have an explicit long-term set of objectives and a clear plan of how to achieve them that we will stay with through thick and thin.

As a confirmed indexer, I realize that indexing is not just right for everyone. For some, the major market value fluctuations are too hard to take. Some of us think differently, and with good reasons, about gains from price changes versus income from dividends. (Personal trusts with income beneficiaries versus remainderman are just one example.)

One major advantage of a dividend focus is that by concentrating on the steady and rising flow of dividends, the investor should be able to reduce the proportion of their portfolio held in bonds in order to moderate ups and downs in the stock market. This, of course, will increase long-term returns and the powers of compounding.

The math of investing is certainly not easy!

Assume nominal returns on stocks are 7%. Fees and taxes will take 1–2%. Inflation will take 2–3%. And then, wham! Behavioral economics—the well-documented costs of making mistakes while striving to "do better"—will take another 2%.

OUCH!

That's why the secret to long-term success in investing is persistence to avoid the great costs of behavioral economics, and the key to persistence is confidence in the people and process that are working for you.

Getting expert help in figuring out what will work best for you is almost always wise. I enjoy the following example: a woman buying a new suit at a major department store can get great advice on the best colors, not where suits are sold, but at the cosmetics counter! Why? Because the "right" color is not the red, blue or green she likes best, but the color that most complements her complexion and the young ladies at the cosmetics counter are experts on complexion complements. Be sure your long-term investment program complements your skills, financial needs, and risk tolerance so you will be able to stay on plan!

FOREWORD

Readers of books on investing have every reason to expect a combination of useful learning and insights into the realities of being in the "combat zone" of making real decisions with real money, and there are plenty of those in this engaging book. Far more important is the chance to learn the core motivations of the people involved.

Every investor owes it to herself or himself to figure out whether a manager sees investing as a business or as a profession, with all the fiduciary characteristics that come from putting clients' interests first. Only skeptics have a chance at getting the true answer. It was my good fortune to serve with Jenny on an investment committee, so I watched her persistent focus on what was right for the client. Readers will find comparable opportunities in this fun and fascinating book to see for themselves the depth of commitment that is at the core of her values.

Charles D. Ellis

Summer, 2024

INTRODUCTION

"An investment in knowledge pays the best interest."
—Benjamin Franklin

Having begun my investment career as the dotcom boom was taking off and high-octane hedge funds were exploding onto the scene, everything pointed toward me becoming a high-flying, high-tech, growth-at-any-cost investor.

While I instantly loved the intrigue and challenge of investing, having grown up in a financially volatile family, aggressive financial risk-taking made me extremely queasy. In 2001, when I inadvertently stumbled into dividend investing, I found a strategy that resonated deep in my core—the comfort, clarity and consistency of a dividend income stream gave me the confidence that I required to be a successful investor. I found it empowering to know that whatever was happening in the mercurial stock market, the income stream that dividends offered would be there chugging along, plunking into investment accounts, providing a reliable source of income month after month.

Only by managing a dividend income portfolio, where the dependability of dividends offered the extraordinary benefit of investment return *and* emotional comfort, could I find the confidence to manage money for other people—money that they had worked so hard to save and that they could either use as a source of income or simply count on as a dependable portion of their total portfolio return.

As with many things in life, my discovery of dividend investing and the true value of a consistent income stream came about by happenstance. At the end of 2001, I was working at Neuberger Berman when a client called in. His name was Steve, and he was a serial entrepreneur who wanted more than anything to spend more time with his truly beautiful wife and three ridiculously fun-loving and interesting sons, all of whom he had wonderful relationships with. Steve's money was being managed in a very S&P 500-esque strategy. He said to me, "Jen, I'm 55 years old, I'm getting ready to retire, so I'll need income; but I know that I am too young to retire, so I will also need growth."

To me, it seemed like an appropriate solution would be to refocus his existing equity portfolio exclusively into stocks with meaningful dividend yields, such that the total portfolio would have an average yield of 5%. While a more traditional approach of investing in bonds and preferred stocks would

INTRODUCTION

have limited Steve's opportunities for long-term capital appreciation, a focus on generating income through the equity exposure kept that door wide open. I described this proposal to Steve as an equity income strategy—a phrase that is commonplace today, but really was not on the radar of most investors 25 years ago.

Steve liked the approach that I had proposed, so we went to work. Well, fast forward a couple of years later and the equity income strategy had exploded! As it turned out, as bond yields fell and then sustained a multi-decade period of low interest rates, many investors really needed sources of consistent income. Certainly, there is no shortage of foundations that need to ensure that their required 5% payout is always available or trusts with obligations to both income and growth beneficiaries. Mostly, however, the equity income strategy makes sense for everyday people.

The individuals that invest in dividend-oriented strategies can be divided into two main categories: those who need income and those who want income.

Those who fall into the "need it" category tend to be focused on a very specific objective—typically the generation of income for retirement or as a supplemental source of funds to support their lifestyle. Perhaps more interesting are the many investors who simply like to see income hitting their portfolios. In the land of unpredictable stock market returns, the monthly deposits of cash from dividends bring tremendous comfort in a frequently discomfiting landscape.

For those who need the income on a regular basis, you might be thinking, "They could just sell positions from their portfolio to generate cash when they need it, right?" The answer is yes, and you are 100% correct in that logic. However, what you will find as you read this book is that psychology is a critical part of investing—both as it affects investors' comfort and confidence in their portfolios and as it impacts stock prices and, in turn, the overall stock market.

While I understood the practical value of a dividend income portfolio from the beginning, it took me a surprisingly long time to conceptualize the true importance of the emotional component of the strategy. Even though the equity income strategy was off to a successful start, and I had left Neuberger Berman in 2006 to move to Gilman Hill Asset Management and essentially go out on my own with the strategy, I did not fully comprehend its unique value until March 5, 2009—just four short days before the S&P 500 hit the diabolical low of 666. I was nine months pregnant at the time and was calling clients to check in and make sure that they were as okay as possible given the market turbulence.

The Goldman Sachs analyst training program had indelibly imprinted on my brain, "When times are tough, you do not hide from your clients." I was not quite three years into having gone out on my own and I felt an overwhelming debt

INTRODUCTION

of obligation and responsibility to the handful of people who had taken a gamble on me and entrusted their life savings to a 30-something-year-old. What would later become known as the bear market of the Great Financial Crisis had started over a year before and the only thing I knew I could do that was guaranteed to be smart was to communicate frequently, openly and honestly.

On March 5, the S&P 500 was down about 60% from its high, which had been set in October 2007. The conversations that I was having basically started with, "Hey, are you okay? So, all bets are off now—I have absolutely no idea what is going to happen next. We could be down more and I can no longer say, 'Well, with history as our guide…'"

One of those calls was to a beloved client, Rick. Rick is an industrial landscaper who inherited a moderately sized trust. He hired me in 2002 to manage his family's investment portfolio. With two kids who were heading off to college, the dividend stream that the trust was generating was a welcome source of additional income for his family.

Fast forward seven years later to 2009, when the world seemed to be melting down… I called up and said, "Hey Rick, are you okay? So, all bets are off right now and I can no longer say, 'Well, with history as our guide…' I have no idea what is going to happen from here. We could easily be down another 10%."

Rick politely cut me off and asked me the most transformative question of my career: "Hey, Jen, are my dividends safe?"

To which I responded, "Yeah, yeah, those are fine; but…"

Rick said—and I remember it clear as day—"Well, if my income is safe, then I'm fine. Don't worry about me. I'm fine!"

Although I had been managing the equity income strategy for about six years at that point, until that moment I did not really understand the simple and critical beauty of this remarkable investment strategy: dividend income provides emotional comfort, emotional comfort encourages good investment behavior and good investment behavior creates superior long-term returns.

Twenty-two years later, this strategy sounds as utterly unremarkable as it did then: invest in a portfolio of stocks that produces a 5% or better aggregate dividend yield. The primary difference between then and now is that back then, almost no one else was doing it. While there are income-oriented strategies aplenty today (many are perfectly sound, but others come with hidden risks in the form of leverage or the excessive use of derivatives to drive the income stream), if you wanted significant dividend income from equities in 2001, you could buy a real estate investment trust (REIT) or utility fund, or you could buy a handful of master limited partnerships (MLPs); but there were very few funds that

INTRODUCTION

focused on dividends. Of course, back in 2001, the ten-year Treasury bond offered an average yield of between 4.5% and 5.5% and the need for income was usually easily satisfied through fixed income—and most individual investors defaulted to that approach.

As our relationship has progressed from 2002 to 2009 to today, the practical and emotional comfort that his dividends provide has helped Rick weather significant bear markets with little discernable anxiety (yes, he is superhuman in that respect). He has seen the S&P 500 return -60% in 2008/2009, -35% in 2020 and -26% in 2022—with many other smaller but still nasty plunges along the way. He has never been forced to sell at the bottom to generate cash because his income has always been there for him and his family, and the comfort of that knowledge has helped him focus on his life and his business without worrying about the temporary whims of the stock market.

In the case of Steve (the serial entrepreneur who gave me the idea to create a dividend stock portfolio in the first place), the income also has served as a remarkable resource for the family. Steve passed away in his sleep a few years ago, at far too young an age. I still manage the portfolio for his wife and often write her notes on her quarterly review that point toward her annual income and her annual withdrawals. The notes often say, "You are underspending! Live it up. Go do something fun!" or—more recently, as she too is finally aging—"Of all the things you have to worry about, money is not one of them. You're okay. Don't worry about this part of your life." The dividends have rolled in and helped set guardrails for the family's spending.

While too many professional investors view portfolio management as a game of performance generation with an index to beat for bragging rights and compensation, I see portfolio management as the pursuit of utilitarian outcomes—be they tangible and/or psychological—for real people. As I often ask my clients, "What is the point of having money if it cannot bring you comfort?" Why else would one save their whole life other than to have a comfortable retirement and/or make their kids' lives a bit more comfortable?

An investment portfolio is worth nothing but the paper that the monthly statements are printed on if it cannot meaningfully improve your life, and hopefully the lives of others. That life improvement can take two primary forms: financial and psychological relief.

As you read this book, please keep Rick's words in mind throughout: "If my income is fine, then I'm fine!" For Rick, the consistent dividend income brings him both financial and emotional comfort.

INTRODUCTION

© Carl Richards.

Now, before you read any further, I would like to point out something that did not actually occur to me until I was 75% finished with the first draft of this book. You will notice that I start each chapter with one of my favorite quotes from some of the investment world's greatest investors. Many of them you will have heard before, as they have become part of the common investment conversation.

Despite coming from different types of investors and wealth creators, and from all eras and centuries, these quotes have one thing in common: they are all about behavior. I find it interesting that the world's best investment advice from the world's best investors is all about behavior—not about how to find a great investment; not about the research process; not about valuation. It seems to be a fair conclusion, then, that excellent investing is very closely correlated with excellent behavior.

And on that note, a final quote to start you off: before there was the 24/7 "wisdom" of financial experts delivered all day long, there was Louis Rukeyser, who hosted a weekly investment show on PBS. In 1996, he interviewed famous investor Philip Carret, the founder of Pioneer Investments, and asked him for his most important piece of investment advice. Mr. Carret answered with one word: "Patience."

I hope that in the pages that follow, you find a strategy or a process that will help you either remain or become a happy, rich old investor.

PART 1

THEORY OF DIVIDEND INVESTING

1
WHAT IS A DIVIDEND?

"Dividends are like plants: Both grow. But dividends can grow forever, while the size of plants is limited."

—Ed Yardeni

What exactly is a *dividend*?

A dividend is a payment, usually made in cash on a regular quarterly basis, to a shareholder. If a stock is trading at $100 per share and has a 5% dividend yield, it means that shareholders will receive $5 per share annually, or $1.25 every three months. So, if you own $1,000 worth of that stock, you will receive $50 per year, or $12.50 each quarter.

If a company has said that it will pay you a $5 dividend, it is likely to do so whether the stock price is $100, $75 or $125. The dividends for most US-based companies are considered fixed and are paid out regularly, and are not affected by the share price. (Later, we will discuss variable dividends.)

If a stock was purchased for $100 with a $5 dividend, then at the time of purchase the dividend yield was 5%. If the market tanks and the shares trade down to $75, but the company is still executing well and continues to pay the $5 dividend, the yield is now 6.7% (5 divided by 75). The opposite is also true: if the market takes off and carries the share price along with it, up to $125 per share, and the company is still happy to pay a $5 dividend, then the dividend yield will now have become 4% (5 divided by 125).

Much more important, however, is the fact that as long as a company does not decrease its annual dividend, an investor can rely on the income that they initially expected from the investment regardless of stock market fluctuations. An additional feather in the cap of dividend income is that in taxable investment accounts, dividends are subject to a favorable tax rate that is usually well below that applied to ordinary income or interest income.

★★★

I recently had an interesting conversation with a potential client who spent his career as an office furniture salesman. He said that he had been managing his own portfolio, but that he knew he wasn't doing a great job even though he should be. I told him that he should come see my office.

Technically, I can and have decorated my own office and have been delighted to do so myself because, well, I am cheap. My office is a hodgepodge of mismatched furniture—all high-

1: WHAT IS A DIVIDEND?

end stuff, but largely acquired piecemeal from this or that business which happened to be selling off its furniture at the time when I needed another desk or filing cabinet. The salesman said, "It probably looks incoherent." Yes, it does—that is exactly the right word.

When I review portfolios for non-professional investors, "incoherent" is usually what I see. Just because I can decorate my office, it doesn't mean that I actually know what I'm doing or understand how to do the job properly. I'm not dumb; it's just a skill that I have not learned. Nor do I have any natural interior decorating instincts.

For better or worse, my do-it-yourself mentality is not limited to office decor. While I am an educated and well-read person, there are many subjects about which I possess just enough knowledge to be dangerous, and many more about which I have no knowledge at all. For example, I truly have no idea how the rules of football work; nor do I care to learn. (I do, thankfully, know that an office needs desks at which its employees can work!)

In the same vein, I often find that even extremely sophisticated, highly capable people do not know the most basic concepts behind how, when and why public companies pay dividends. And why should they? I know that calamine lotion helps soothe poison ivy rash, but how? I haven't the foggiest idea. For a chemist, botanist or biologist, I am sure that this is as basic as it gets; but for me? No clue.

So why do companies pay dividends instead of just keeping all the cash? One reason is that in order to entice people to buy its stock, a company needs to offer potential shareholders something in return. For some companies, that enticement is the *prospect* of enormous future growth in earnings and, hopefully, in share price. For others, it is the *promise* of a regular return on the money that a shareholder has invested in that company.

Companies may also pay and regularly increase dividends as a way to signal their confidence in the future, as well as their control of the business's financial prospects and balance sheet. Paying stable and growing dividends is a way to advertise to potential shareholders, "Come invest with us—we know what we're doing and know how to return money to our investors. In a sea of knuckleheads, we're the mature grownup who can actually run a significantly profitable company."

Let's think about this more specifically with the example of Chevron. In 1878, Chevron (a descendant of Standard Oil) was a company with explosive growth potential. The discovery of oil—"black gold," as they called it back then—was new and the growth in demand was huge. Drilling wells, laying pipeline and building refineries were expensive activities; and as Chevron made money, it reinvested the capital into the business to continue growing and keep up with the insatiable demand for oil. Then, gradually, once everyone and everything in the world seemed to be fully dependent on petroleum products and millions of barrels of oil were being consumed daily, the *rate* of growth slowed and Chevron no longer needed to reinvest such a big percentage of its earnings back into the business in order to drive new revenue growth. As Chevron matured, it found itself with billions and billions of excess cash each year. So, what did it do? It decided to return the cash to its shareholders in the form of dividends.

Figure 1.1: Chevron share price and dividend (DPS) growth (1973–2024)

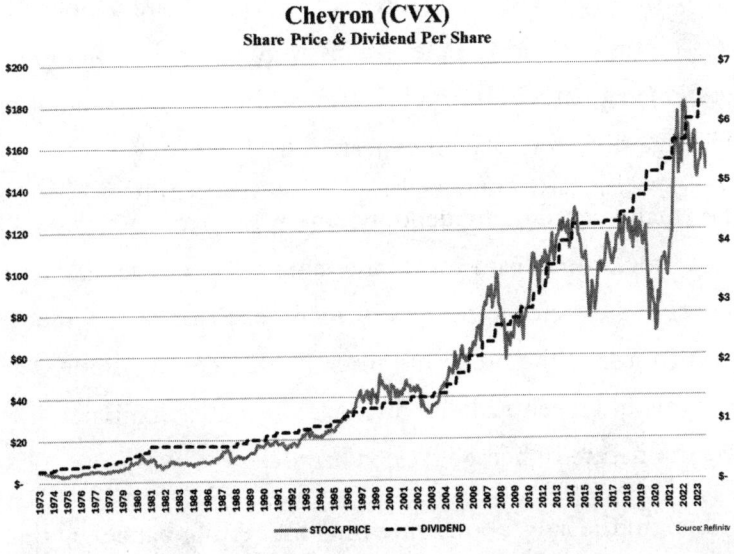

Over time, companies like Chevron discovered that returning cash to shareholders in the form of a consistently paid-out dividend added value and cachet to their stocks. Corporations understand that consistent dividend payments telegraph to investors that management have competent and skillful control over the business. Most serious dividend-paying companies are extremely careful to set a dividend policy that can survive even the worst-case recessions. Chevron, for example, sets its dividend policy to survive a ten-year period in which oil may trade between $20 and $150 per barrel. Other well-managed dividend-paying companies put similar stress tests in place before they issue or increase their dividends.

In the United States, companies that pay dividends usually do so on a quarterly basis. (Overseas, dividends are frequently less consistent and lumpier.) This is good for corporations' cash management planning, as well as for investors' ability to manage their own return expectations.

For many decades, dividend income was prized by investors, and stocks that paid large and consistent dividends were cherished as reliable sources of income. Prior to the 1990s, an investor in the broad US stock market could assume that they would receive a hefty dividend payout each quarter, just by the nature of being invested in stocks.

Then, in the late 1990s, something interesting happened that changed corporate capital allocation behavior. Technology began to BOOM. For the first time, companies that paid dividends came to be viewed as "old economy." Hotshot "new economy" stocks, on the other hand, were expected to reinvest every cent that they earned into their businesses,

1: WHAT IS A DIVIDEND?

based on the assumption that growth prospects were essentially infinite in the internet era. This wholesale reinvestment back into the company was referred to as "enterprise building." While enterprise building worked for some companies, like Apple and Microsoft, the lack of capital discipline that it sparked also led to many failures, most of which we don't even remember (Ciena, ValueClick and Geocities were a few).

Reflecting this new mindset, during the 1990s, the yield on the S&P 500 dropped from a 3%–3.5% range to as low as 1.11% in 2000. Indeed, it has spent most of the 2000s under 2%. At the same time, interest rates also came down dramatically (the ten-year US Treasury bond fell from 6%–7% in 1995 to an average of 2.4% from 2010–2023) and the US population, led by the baby boomers, started to age and retire. As this population retired and began to rely increasingly on their investments to support themselves, dividend-paying stocks remained a critical source of income. However, unlike periods prior to the 1990s, when just investing in the broad market was enough to generate significant dividend income, investors now needed to seek out dedicated dividend-paying stocks and investment strategies.

Today, we are seeing a renewed focus on dividend return to shareholders. In 2022, the total dividends paid out by S&P 500 companies was $565 billion, the highest figure on record. For the first time in decades, interest rates are structurally higher and near-zero borrowing costs seem to be a phenomenon of yesteryear. Also, in the four years from 2018 to 2022, investors experienced three bear markets (as defined by a 20% or more market decline). As their revenues and market capitalizations have reached gargantuan scale, the Apples and Microsofts of the world have become so mature and so profitable that their future growth rate prospects have significantly diminished (much like what happened to Chevron decades earlier). Meanwhile, they are enormously profitable and generate more cash than they can possibly reinvest in their businesses. So, what are they doing? They are paying dividends. In fact, in 2023, Microsoft was the world's single-largest dividend payer, returning approximately $19 billion to shareholders. (However, because of the high valuation of the share price, the dividend yield on Microsoft shares is still under 1%.)

As we move into the second quarter of the 21st century—which is likely to be characterized by potentially slower economic growth but enormous profitability for the mega-scale companies—it seems probable that companies like Apple and Microsoft are poised to follow the path of Chevron by offering more and more dividend income to shareholders. And as the population continues to age, it is likely that the demand for this dividend income to supplement or support retirement will add additional pressure on companies to pay out their excess cash to shareholders. For dividend investors, this refreshing of the dividend income well is a happy reality that plays out on an evolutionary basis over time.

1: WHAT IS A DIVIDEND?

Interestingly, over just the past decade, we have witnessed leadership shifts and dramatic growth in the dividends paid by some of the world's largest companies (see Table 1.1).

Table 1.1: Top ten dividend payers in the S&P 500 and values ($ billions) of dividends paid

2023		2018		2013	
Microsoft (MSFT)	$19	Apple (AAPL)	$14	ExxonMobil (XOM)	$11
Apple (AAPL)	$15	ExxonMobil (XOM)	$14	Apple (AAPL)	$11
ExxonMobil (XOM)	$15	Microsoft (MSFT)	$13	AT&T (T)	$10
JPMorgan Chase (JPM)	$13	AT&T (T)	$12	Microsoft (MSFT)	$9
Johnson & Johnson (JNJ)	$12	Johnson & Johnson (JNJ)	$10	Chevron (CVX)	$8
Chevron (CVX)	$11	Verizon (VZ)	$10	Johnson & Johnson (JNJ)	$7
Verizon (VZ)	$11	Chevron (CVX)	$9	General Electric (GE)	$7
Procter & Gamble (PG)	$9	JPMorgan Chase (JPM)	$8	Procter & Gamble (PG)	$7
Coca-Cola (KO)	$8	Wells Fargo (WFC)	$8	Pfizer (PFE)	$7
AT&T (T)	$8	Procter & Gamble (PG)	$7	Walmart (WMT)	$6

As we move into the coming decades, it is most likely that collectively, US companies will continue to pay out enormous sums of their income in the form of dividends. However, the leadership of the biggest dividend payers and the amounts they pay will always fluctuate and evolve.

2
EMOTIONAL COMFORT

> "The investor's chief problem—and his worst enemy—is likely to be himself. In the end, how your investments behave is much less important than how you behave."
> —Benjamin Graham

INVESTING for dividend income can provide an investor with the warm, cozy blanket of reliable cash in their pockets through thick and thin. The comfort of knowing that you do not need to make an active decision to sell stocks for cash to be deposited in your investment account—regardless of a bull or bear market; regardless of if you are hard at work at the office, relaxing at home or on a cruise in the middle of the ocean—can be immensely useful and, I believe, encourages the type of superior investment behavior that correlates to excellent long-term investment returns.

Just about anyone who has ever worked with an investment advisor will have had the talk about staying invested in order not to miss the market's best days (see Table 2.1). Most people also have seen the data that shows the difference between the average individual investor's ten-year return of

8.7% versus the S&P 500's return of 16.6% (Figure 2.1) and then received the explanation that the difference is a factor of behavior.

If you have seen either or both of these many times over, the reason is because they are true. And the claim that there is that big a difference between the individual and the S&P 500 due to emotions—well, that is also true.

Table 2.1: Stay invested vs. missing the best days
Return on $10,000 invested in the S&P 500 (ten years ending July 2024)

S&P 500 Total Return, 10 Years ending 7/31/24	Annualized Return	Ending Value of $10,000 invested
Miss 10 Worst Days	20.7%	$65,803.93
Miss 5 Worst Days	18.0%	$52,364.41
Miss Worst Day	14.6%	$39,085.52
All Days	13.2%	$34,403.15
Miss Best Day	12.1%	$31,448.99
Miss Best 5 Days	9.1%	$23,865.35
Miss Best 10 Days	6.5%	$18,827.43

2: EMOTIONAL COMFORT

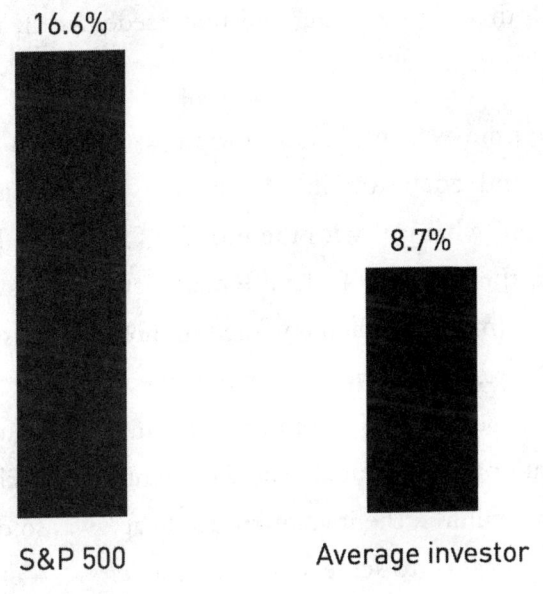

Figure 2.1: Ten-year annualized returns (2012–2021)

- S&P 500: 16.6%
- Average investor: 8.7%

Source: J.P. Morgan.

However, there is a big difference between knowing what the right thing to do is and actually being able to do it. I, for one, eat far more than my share of doughnuts and chocolate croissants for breakfast. They are just so delicious; and when choosing between plain yogurt with granola and a chocolate croissant or custard-filled, chocolate-frosted doughnut, the less healthy option usually gets the better of me.

The stock market holds these same temptations. Think back to March 2009 or March 2020, when the S&P 500 bottomed out at the respective bear market lows. Try to remember (or imagine) how you felt at those times. In my career, those were the only times that I have been truly scared. In both instances, I was no longer able to rely on market history as a guide. Both were terrifying and unprecedented in modern history.

The last time we saw banks collapse at the same level as in 2008 and 2009 was in March 1933 during the Great Depression (what is it with the month of March?!). In 1933, however, there was no Federal Reserve and very few social safety nets (most of which emerged in direct response to the Great Depression). Trading was not effected electronically; the US economy was dominated by manufacturing; and globalization was essentially non-existent. So, while there were bank failures, the investment landscape was so different that history failed to serve as a useful guide.

When, on March 9, 2009, the US stock market bottomed out at down 57% from its previous peak, many people who had been invested in stocks saw portfolios that may have started at $1 million touch down as low as $530,000. This, of course, was truly terrifying for people who were relying on those portfolios to support what they had hoped would be a comfortable retirement; and for those of us responsible for managing portfolios amid a stock market that had become untethered from rationality and historical context.

Similarly, during the early days of the Covid-19 pandemic, the only other time that seemed relevant was the Spanish flu pandemic of 1918. Information flow, healthcare and technology, however, had changed so much in the preceding century that we had no truly similar time period for comparison. As the S&P plunged by 34% from its peak in the course of a few weeks, people saw their $1 million portfolios collapse to $660,000. Not only were their savings bludgeoned, but they couldn't leave their homes, go to work or send their kids to school. Trips were canceled, graduation celebrations canceled, weddings canceled. In many ways, 2020 was even more terrifying than 2009 because the fear permeated our entire lives—physical, social, professional and financial.

The point of reminding you of this fear is to think back to how hard it was to see your investment account plunging in an environment with extremely little visibility. While we all know that we should try to avoid panic selling when the market is going down, and that we should, according to Warren Buffett, "Be fearful when others are greedy and greedy when others are fearful," acting on that logic and not acting on the emotional fear instinct is very difficult.

So what on earth are investors supposed to do?!

In my 25-plus years of managing a dividend income strategy, I have found that the reliability of dividend income is remarkably useful in supporting good investment behavior in exactly these worst-case scenario situations. Because it means that you do not need to sell into the teeth of a bear market to generate the cash on which you depend, dividend income keeps you invested—which is the correct thing to do at times when the market and your emotional state are telling you to do the opposite.

Consider the following two situations.

Maria has a $1 million portfolio that is invested for dividend income. She is a retired journalist and during her working years she saved prudently for a very, very long time. Her portfolio produces $40,000 of income per year and that supplements her $36,000 a year from social security. Of critical importance here is that Maria will never be forced to sell her stocks to generate the $40,000 of income that she needs to live on. Whether the stock market is at a high or low point, she will never be forced to sell stocks at the wrong time—or even to make a decision. The dividend income will just flow into her portfolio.

Allison has a $500,000 portfolio that is invested in growth stocks with a stock market-like dividend yield which produces about $7,500 per year of income. Allison is an engineer working for a multinational industrial firm. She is not focused on the income and would like to see this portfolio grow significantly so that one day she'll have a couple million dollars saved up.

Now, let's say that it is March 2020 and things are really dark and scary. Let's assume that both portfolios are down 34% because of the stock market drop. Let's consider the

2: EMOTIONAL COMFORT

internal dialogs that these two investors might have with themselves:

Maria: If I sell now, my income will cease. I know that many of the companies that I am invested in have paid dividends for decades; many of them continued to pay through the Great Financial Crisis as well as the huge drop in oil prices in 2015/16 and the mini-bear market in 2018. I really need that $40,000 of extra income and as long as people keep living, I know that the companies that I am invested in will keep earning money and paying out dividends. I know what the value of my companies is because I can see what the future cash flow payments to me, the investor, are likely to be. Thank goodness I don't need to sell my stocks when they're all down so much, or make a decision at a time of stress and confusion, in order to generate cash to cover my expenses!

Allison: This market is really scary and could easily go down more. If I sell now, I may be able to buy all my stocks back cheaper when I know that the bottom is in. Mostly, though, I am really scared and if I want to get my portfolio to $2 million by the time I retire, I cannot afford to lose another penny from here. I don't have any idea what the real value of these companies is because it's based on what other investors are willing to pay, which is ultimately an emotional decision—in good times investors are willing to pay a high multiple on expected future earnings and in bad times they simply are not. I'm out for now. [Note to the reader: almost no one actually gets back in at the bottom, because by then the fear has increased. In my experience with this situation, the investor only gets back in after the market has dramatically improved. By reinvesting after the world starts to feel like a better place and stocks have shown positive improvement, a significant amount of portfolio value is permanently lost due to missing out on the market's initial bounce-back off a bear-market bottom.]

There is a famous old story (it may be apocryphal, and I have been unable to verify it) about Peter Lynch, one of the most successful portfolio managers of all time. When Mr. Lynch was managing Fidelity's Magellan Fund, the marketing department came to him and said, "Mr. Lynch, the average investor in the Magellan Fund has lost money." He responded, "That's impossible. I know what my returns are, and they are overwhelmingly positive—better than the market! Please go back and recalculate your findings." They did and returned with the answer, "Our numbers are correct and the average holding period in the Magellan Fund is ten months." Lack of patience led to poor behavior, which led to the shortening of investment timeframes and thus losses instead of gains in the venerable Magellan Fund for the average investor.

2: EMOTIONAL COMFORT

Without a doubt, the most important element of an individual's investment success is behavior. Professional investors are trained to control their behavior and may succeed using a variety of different investment strategies. Individuals, while highly trained in their unique professions, are likely to be less comfortable seeing their investment dollars flung about by the whims of the stock market and may find that a strategy where the cash just rolls in regularly—very much like their bi-weekly paychecks—brings them the comfort that they need to stick it out through a variety of market environments.

3

WHAT TYPES OF COMPANIES CHOOSE TO PAY DIVIDENDS AND WHY?

"I think you have to learn that there's a company behind every stock, and that there's only one real reason why stocks go up. Companies go from doing poorly to doing well or small companies grow to large companies."

—Peter Lynch

IF you are reading this book—and, by the way, thank you very much for reading this book!—you have probably heard of the Dividend Aristocrats. This is a list of 68 companies that have all paid and raised their dividends for 25 or more consecutive years. Perhaps surprisingly, you will notice that most of the companies that qualify as a Dividend Aristocrat do not actually have a particularly high dividend yield. In fact, as a point of reference, the dividend yield of the S&P 500 has been around 1.7% for most of the past decade!

Table 3.1 presents a list of the Dividend Aristocrats as of May 2024.

Table 3.1: Dividend Aristocrats (May 2024)

Name	Ticker	Dividend yield	Years of dividend increases
3M Co.	MMM	6.60%	66
A.O. Smith Corp.	AOS	1.60%	30
Abbott Laboratories	ABT	1.90%	52
Abbvie Inc.	ABBV	3.50%	52
Aflac Inc.	AFL	2.50%	42
Air Products & Chemicals Inc.	APD	3.10%	42
Albemarle Corp.	ALB	1.30%	28
Amcor Plc★	AMCR	5.40%	4
Archer Daniels Midland Co.	ADM	3.70%	51
Atmos Energy Corp.	ATO	2.80%	40
Automatic Data Processing Inc.	ADP	2.20%	49
Becton Dickinson & Co.	BDX	1.50%	52
Brown & Brown, Inc.	BRO	0.60%	30
Brown-Forman Corp.	BF.B	1.50%	40
C.H. Robinson Worldwide, Inc.	CHRW	3.40%	25
Cardinal Health, Inc.	CAH	1.90%	36
Caterpillar Inc.	CAT	1.60%	30
Chevron Corp.	CVX	4.20%	37
Chubb Limited	CB	1.40%	31
Church & Dwight Co., Inc.	CHD	1.20%	28
Cincinnati Financial Corp.	CINF	2.90%	64
Cintas Corporation	CTAS	0.90%	41

3: WHAT TYPES OF COMPANIES CHOOSE TO PAY DIVIDENDS AND WHY?

Name	Ticker	Dividend yield	Years of dividend increases
Clorox Co.	CLX	3.10%	46
Coca-Cola Co.	KO	3.20%	62
Colgate-Palmolive Co.	CL	2.30%	61
Consolidated Edison, Inc.	ED	3.70%	50
Dover Corp.	DOV	1.30%	68
Ecolab, Inc.	ECL	1.10%	32
Emerson Electric Co.	EMR	2.00%	67
Essex Property Trust, Inc.	ESS	3.90%	29
Expeditors International Of Washington, Inc.	EXPD	1.20%	28
Exxon Mobil Corp.	XOM	3.60%	41
Fastenal Co.	FAST	2.20%	25
Federal Realty Investment Trust	FRT	4.40%	56
Franklin Resources, Inc.	BEN	4.60%	44
General Dynamics Corp.	GD	1.90%	32
Genuine Parts Co.	GPC	2.80%	68
Hormel Foods Corp.	HRL	3.80%	58
Illinois Tool Works, Inc.	ITW	2.20%	60
International Business Machines Corp.	IBM	3.70%	29
J.M. Smucker Co.	SJM	3.40%	27
Johnson & Johnson	JNJ	3.00%	61
Kenvue Inc.	KVUE	4.10%	61
Kimberly-Clark Corp.	KMB	4.10%	52
Leggett & Platt, Inc.	LEG	9.00%	52

Name	Ticker	Dividend yield	Years of dividend increases
Linde plc	LIN	1.20%	30
Lowe's Cos., Inc.	LOW	1.90%	60
McCormick & Co., Inc.	MKC	2.50%	38
McDonald's Corp.	MCD	2.30%	47
Medtronic plc	MDT	3.20%	46
NextEra Energy Inc.	NEE	3.30%	28
Nordson Corp.	NDSN	1.00%	60
Nucor Corp.	NUE	1.20%	51
Pentair plc	PNR	1.20%	48
PepsiCo Inc.	PEP	3.20%	52
PPG Industries, Inc.	PPG	1.80%	52
Procter & Gamble Co.	PG	2.30%	67
Realty Income Corp.	O	5.80%	26
Roper Technologies Inc.	ROP	0.50%	31
S&P Global Inc.	SPGI	0.90%	51
Sherwin-Williams Co.	SHW	0.90%	46
Stanley Black & Decker Inc.	SWK	3.70%	56
Sysco Corp.	SYY	2.50%	53
T. Rowe Price Group Inc.	TROW	4.50%	38
Target Corp.	TGT	3.00%	55
W.W. Grainger Inc.	GWW	0.80%	52
Walmart Inc.	WMT	1.30%	50
West Pharmaceutical Services, Inc.	WST	0.20%	31

* Amcor merged with Bemis in 2019, but its history of dividend increases goes back more than 25 years, hence its inclusion here.

Just because a company pays a dividend does not mean that it intends to have the dividend income be a major component of shareholders' total return. Some companies, like Realty Income Trust, focus on creating significant income for their shareholders and maintain dividend yields that are well above the market average, and are thus considered dividend income stocks.

However, most of the Dividend Aristocrats are more like Procter & Gamble (P&G) and Walmart: they have much lower dividend yields, but still focus on growing their earnings significantly and maintaining growth in their dividends. These are considered dividend growth companies.

For investors looking for their portfolios to produce a meaningful stream of income, dividend income stocks are where it's at.

Why does one company opt to pay out a large, above-market dividend yield while another does not?

Let's consider the example of Realty Income Trust—a triple-net lease REIT that owns properties leased by tenants like CVS Pharmacies, 7-Eleven and BJ's Wholesale Clubs. The properties are leased out on very long-term contracts, often about 20 years. The tenants are responsible for everything, including maintenance, taxes and improvements (thus, "triple-net lease"). This means the owners of the properties have extremely resilient and transparent future revenue and profit streams, but with minimal growth prospects outside of the obligatory annual rent escalators that were established at the start of the lease agreement. Triple-net lease businesses are very formulaic: they borrow money at a lower interest rate than the rate of return they expect to make off the rental of the property, collect the rental cash, pay out most of their income to shareholders, rinse and repeat. Banks are happy to lend at favorable rates when the profitability of a project is transparent. The returns are moderate, but the certainty of success is very high.

P&G, on the other hand, sells everything from Gillette razors to Pampers and Dawn dish detergent. The way P&G drives growth in its business is through constant product innovation and marketing. Unlike Realty Income Trust, P&G needs to use its cash for continuous investment in product innovation, which has a very high but less predictable return on investment (think about how there is always a newer and better version of a razor coming out with a newer and better advertising campaign). So, while P&G uses a significant amount of its cash flow to reinvest in products that will drive the future growth of earnings, it also knows that after all its business investments, there will still be a large amount of cash left over. It understands that P&G shareholders rely on some part of their investment return being "a bird in the hand," or a reliable plunk of cash into their investment account each quarter.

Figure 3.1 shows the consistency with which P&G has paid and raised its dividend dating all the way back to 1975. Interestingly, it also highlights that while both the share price and the dividend are on an upward trajectory, the upward trajectory of the dividend is significantly more consistent.

Figure 3.1: Procter & Gamble share price and dividend (DPS) growth (1975–2024)

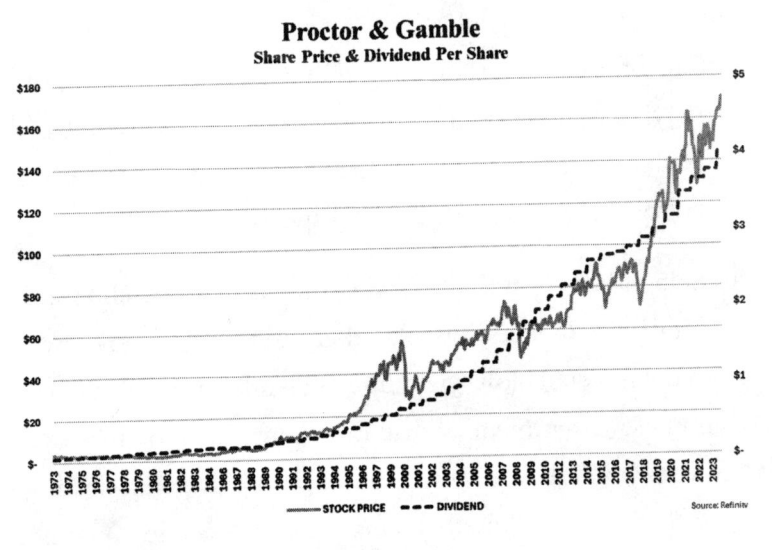

Proctor & Gamble
Share Price & Dividend Per Share

[Chart showing stock price and dividend from 1973 to 2023, with stock price on left axis ($0-$180) and dividend on right axis ($0-$5). Source: Refinitiv]

In addition to knowing that their shareholders require some part of their return to be predictable, companies like P&G (as well as Exxon, IBM, etc.) have a precedent problem. Even if their management teams and boards of directors begin to consider that it is a poor capital allocation decision to pay out such a substantial amount of cash as a dividend, rather than investing it back in their own business, if they decided to stop paying a dividend or even just to reduce the dividend, they would have a shareholder revolt and an investor relations nightmare on their hands.

Management also must take into consideration the fact that dividend cuts frequently (but not always) reflect poorly on investor perceptions of how well a company is being managed. As mentioned earlier, in the United States, a consistently paid dividend has come to signal the health of a company and the strong control of the business by management. The cutting of a dividend, on the other hand, generally signals underlying financial problems and/or mistakes by company leadership; and more often than not, it is regarded as a bad omen for the company's future prospects.

To help us better understand why some companies choose to pay out large dividends, while others do not, let's move away from the generally low-yielding Dividend Aristocrats list and examine two companies that my clients have owned over the years and are in the same business of equipment leasing: growth-focused United Rentals and dividend income-focused H&E Equipment (H&E).

United Rentals, based in Stamford, Connecticut, is an equipment leasing company that rents everything from forklifts and excavators to air compressors and towable lights. It was formed in 1997 and became a publicly traded company within just three months. The company was created by serial entrepreneur Brad Jacobs, who had built five companies from the ground up—all of which became billion-dollar-plus enterprises and three of which became publicly traded companies (United Rentals and XPO Logistics are the two that Jacobs is most famous for). From the beginning, the growth of United Rentals was driven by acquisition. When Jacobs decided to create an equipment rental business, what he saw was an opportunity to consolidate highly fragmented industry-dominated small local equipment lessors and mom-and-pop businesses. The equipment leasing process was manual and time intensive. He saw an opportunity to essentially roll up and modernize the equipment leasing business through the use of scale and technology.

Baton Rouge-based H&E, on the other hand, was founded in 1961 by Tom Enquist and Frank Head. Indeed, the company's original name was Head & Enquist. Head was a Houston-based equipment distributor and Enquist was a manufacturer's sales rep. The two men saw an opportunity to lease construction equipment to the booming Houston/Louisiana/Sunbelt region and grew the company almost entirely organically. There were natural management changes along the way and a merger with ICM Equipment Company in 2002, which is when the company's name changed from Head & Enquist to H&E Equipment Services LLC. However, even today, the Enquist family remains firmly involved, with John M. Enquist (Tom's son) and John Enquist (Tom's grandson) serving as executive chairman, president and chief operating officer respectively.

So, here we have two companies that essentially have the same business: construction equipment rentals. The geographies are different, but as each has grown, there has been more and more overlap and geographic contingency. Thankfully, the need for construction equipment has boomed and both businesses have remained extremely profitable. Everything from Hurricanes Harvey and Ian to the vast expansion of US oil and gas production in areas from the Permian Basin in the Southwest to the Marcellus Shale in the Northeast has created significant demand for both companies. Investment in highways and housing development has also pushed demand. Both companies have been major beneficiaries of this growth.

From an investment perspective, there is one key area where the companies diverge dramatically: capital allocation. United Rentals, which was founded to essentially roll up a fragmented and inefficient industry, believed that the best use of its enormous free cash flow generation was to buy up competitors to drive growth through acquisition. H&E, meanwhile, was created to supply rental equipment to construction projects and to generate income for the original Head and Enquist families. In its early years, the company was essentially a family-run business and believed that returning a large dividend to shareholders (the two families and other employees of the company were significant shareholders) was a critical element of the value proposition that it was able to offer investors.

3: WHAT TYPES OF COMPANIES CHOOSE TO PAY DIVIDENDS AND WHY?

The comparison of H&E and United Rentals offers a valuable reminder that any type of company can pay dividends, and that each decision-making process is unique and complex. Frequently, people assume that certain companies either do or do not pay a strong dividend based on nothing more than the industry in which the company operates. It is true that REITs and midstream energy companies, due to their tax structures, generally fit the stereotype and tend to pay out significant dividend income. As a result of their high cash flow generation and low growth prospects, utilities have also correctly fallen into the high dividend payer stereotype. However, outside of those groups, paying a dividend is a choice, not a presumption, and the decision is often made very strategically by the board of directors and management. Sometimes, offering a large dividend can be used as a tool to attract a shareholder base that shares the same values of consistent cash flow generation and is supportive of a management team that will consistently try to hit singles and doubles, and not swing for the fences with the aspiration of a rare grand slam. Coincidentally, shareholders that value dividends are frequently more long-term focused and less rabblerouser-activist in nature, and in many cases make for a better shareholder partnership with a company's leadership team.

Interestingly, in early 2024, two companies that no one had pinned as dividend payers each initiated dividends: Meta and Salesforce. After a long run as ultra-high-growth technology companies, both found themselves in the position of having become enormous generators of free cash flow and the question arose as to how this excess cash would be best allocated. Both companies had histories of making acquisitions, but by 2024 there were no acquisitions that were compelling or largescale enough to be a good use for their cash piles. Both decided to buy back shares and issue dividends.

A quick aside on buybacks versus dividends: theoretically, issuing dividends and buying back stock are both ways to return cash to shareholders. However, one method is direct and the other is indirect. In the case of dividends, the cash literally is deposited into a shareholder's brokerage account each quarter. In the case of share buybacks, the number of a company's shares are reduced, which directly increases the earnings per share. Theoretically, the shares should then trade higher, since there are now more earnings per share than there were when there was a greater number of shares outstanding. Whether or not the shares respond accordingly, however, is largely down to the whims of the market.

In the United States, the regularity of expected dividend payments is viewed as sacrosanct. Once a company starts paying a dividend, unless it was originally announced as a "special" one-time dividend, it is presumed that dividends will be paid quarterly and will show regular growth. Share buybacks, on the other hand, are expected to be more ad hoc in nature, whereby a company buys back shares when it is flush with cash and does not when cash is scarcer. Theoretically, share buybacks are a better use of capital allocation in that they increase the per-share profitability of a company. Practically, however, investors love seeing cash dropped into their brokerage accounts and value the immediate return of a dividend versus the more indirect return of a share buyback. Psychologically, companies that pay dividends are also thought of as safety plays, based on the idea that if a company is generating so much excess cash that it can confidently expect to pay a consistent dividend well into the future, then it must have a secure future. So, in addition to being a practical way to offer compelling shareholder return, a dividend acts as a signal of corporate strength and stability.

Now, let's return to Meta and Salesforce. As it turns out, Mark Zuckerberg and Marc Benioff, the respective CEOs, are large owners of their respective companies' stock. Yes, they are gazillionaires, and no, they probably have not been pinched for cash in the past two decades; but they also are stuck with only two ways to monetize their Meta and Salesforce stock—sell shares or pay out cash through a dividend. Like the Enquist family, which was still heavily invested in H&E when the company went public and started paying a dividend, it seems likely that Zuckerberg and Benioff simply enjoy seeing dollars from their stock holdings drop into their brokerage accounts each quarter. No matter how rich someone is, it seems that human nature is to love cash, and we see that many dividend-paying companies have significant management, family and founding family ownership.

As was mentioned previously, for companies in the United States, dividend payments are expected to be regular and once a company starts paying a dividend, it is on the hook to keep paying a dividend. Interestingly, however, overseas, dividends do not have the same presumption of regularity and consistency. In fact, many foreign companies pay dividends with less consistency and less regularity. Elsewhere, dividends are often viewed in the way that share buybacks are in the United States—as bonuses when there is plenty of extra cash, not as a guaranteed, eternal promise. Since they were never established as something regular or guaranteed, cutting and raising dividends for overseas companies does not raise eyebrows the way they would in the United States.

Figure 3.2: S&P 500 index dividend yield (1985–2023)

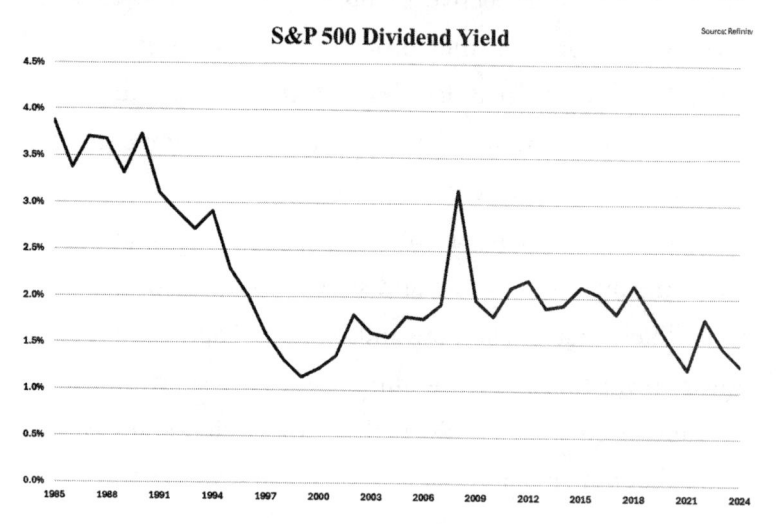

S&P 500 Dividend Yield

Source: Refinitiv

PART 2

THE PRACTICE OF DIVIDEND INVESTING

4
SCREENING

> "Supremely rational investors take the further step of acting against consensus, rebalancing to long-term portfolio targets by buying the out-of-favor and selling the in-vogue."
> —*David F. Swensen*

ONE of the most important yet difficult to overcome elements of successful investing is suppressing subjectivity and prioritizing objectivity. I have always found that using a screening process to source investment ideas and encourage objectivity is critical. With around one-third of the companies in the Russell 3000 paying a dividend, a screen is the most effective way to begin to figure out which companies may warrant future investment.

The challenge here for the individual investor is that screening is a heck of a lot easier for professionals with expensive software and detailed data feeds at their fingertips

Many portfolio managers use a screen, and their screens come in every flavor and variety. My preferred screen is extremely basic and has, for over 20 years, helped me to source unique ideas and make excellent investment decisions.

So, I will describe mine; but please do not think that this is the only way to do it. The best part of a screen is that it forces objectivity and discipline—two of the most critical components for good investing.

Professional investors use resources like LSEG, Bloomberg and Factset. For non-professional dividend investors, access to comprehensive and accurate databases is harder to come by, and resources such as local libraries, custodian resources or low-cost online screening services may need to be availed of.

Here is how I run my screen:

- I set the parameters to look for all publicly traded companies in the United States with the following characteristics:
  - A dividend yield of over 3.5%; and
  - A market capitalization of over $150 million.
- While I do not screen companies on these criteria, I include the following useful information:
  - Sector and industry (my primary sorting criterion);
  - Historical earnings and dividend growth rates;
  - Earnings and dividend per share (so that I can see how well the dividend is covered by the earnings);
  - Price-to-earnings multiple (current and forward); and
  - Leverage ratios.

For REITs and MLPs, the enormous depreciation generated by their assets renders "earnings" a useless metric. Therefore, for REITs, I look at funds from operations;

4: SCREENING

while for MLPs, cash available for distribution is a more realistic measure of the company's earnings generation.
- The following are automatically eliminated:
  - Companies that I have recently researched and definitively decided against; and
  - Mortgage REITs, because I have learned that the dividends are at risk in a distorted interest rate environment, and I seek companies that can pay dividends regardless of broader economic turmoil.
- A fun tip that enhances the screening process is the use of color coding. It may seem silly, but I color code everything I already own in green. Yellow is for stocks that I have already researched but have not yet bought. Previously owned companies are orange; companies I am unlikely to ever own are color coded in brown; and so on. The visual aid of color coding helps make the plethora of investment choices that your screen may reveal seem a lot less daunting.

Again, the most critical element of using a screen is the discipline it brings, forcing you to stay objective and look at companies that you might not otherwise know or think about, and to reevaluate outdated or preconceived notions when stocks move up or down the objective screen.

Running the screen narrows the pool from about 3,000 companies to a few hundred. It is from this winnowed list that I start to identify investable opportunities.

The next step in selecting appropriate securities for investment is to consider the dividend payment history. Sometimes, a company will suddenly appear on the screen with a juicy dividend, but the three- or five-year history of the company's dividend growth will reveal it is a special or one-time dividend, with no expectation for future dividend payments. Other times, a long and steady history of paying a dividend will be revealed—this is what I am looking for!

Take, for example, a recent addition to my portfolio: Stanley Black & Decker. Stanley is a Dividend Aristocrat, but it had never appeared on my weekly screen prior to 2023. Despite paying and raising the dividend for over 50 years, the share price had consistently been high enough that the dividend yield was always under my 3.5% hurdle. That changed as a result of the Covid-19 pandemic, when everyone and their brother decided to move out of cities, buy homes and embrace the DIY lifestyle. Stanley benefited hugely from this trend. Shares surged in anticipation of earnings surging, which they did. But then, supply chains became seriously screwed up and inventories followed suit. Several years' worth of sales had essentially been pulled forward and, as the world began to normalize again, revenues declined—which, compounded by inventory problems, caused earnings to plunge. As always seems to be the case, the share price responded violently and dropped by 60%.

As a result, in late 2022, Stanley suddenly appeared on my weekly screen. If it weren't for the forced objectivity of the screen, I never would have known that Stanley was now within my sights. Certainly, I would not have thought to myself, "Hey, I wonder what Stanley's share price is doing nowadays?" Maybe I would have seen the company at a conference and realized that the yield had crept up. Potentially *Barron's* or *Forbes* would have written an article and I might have noticed. Unless the title of an industry research report had blared, "Stanley Dividend Above 3.5%," I may not have read it. And anyway, any of those triggers would have meant that I was late to the party in recognizing that an opportunity may be presenting itself.

Using an objective screen that is run very regularly allows investors to be early to the party when a new potential investment is developing. In the case of Stanley, when it first appeared on the weekly screen, I lightly began the initial research process just to find out why it was appearing on the screen. Had it raised the dividend so that the yield was higher? Or had the shares fallen while the company maintained the dividend, thus rendering the yield higher?

The ability to spend significant time on conducting a thorough research process is a great advantage (and also frequently just not possible, because sometimes stock prices move way too fast), but running a regular screen often allows for the early identification of new developments.

In the case of Stanley, I was able to avoid a fire-drill research process and begin a thorough, thoughtful, humanely paced process that ended up spanning several months and allowed me to think deeply about what had gone on, piece together a valuation framework and decide at what price I would be willing to purchase the shares. From there, I was able to sit back and let the share price continue to come to me until it reached a level where I was willing to invest.

Screens are not only a critical component of sourcing ideas and maintaining an objective investment process, but also a lot of fun! Each week, looking through a fresh new screen is almost like going on a treasure hunt. Sorting through the various sectors for potential new investment companies is both interesting and enlightening—sometimes there will be lots of opportunity in the energy sector, while other times the consumer discretionary sector may offer the greatest potential. The real estate sector is always fertile, while healthcare vacillates. After years of sorting through screens, many companies become familiar old acquaintances, making the occasional find of something new and truly compelling a welcome little thrill!

5
RESEARCHING DIVIDEND COMPANIES

"If you can eliminate a few disasters, compounding will take care of the rest."

—*Charles D. Ellis*

While risk and the potential loss of capital are always a reality when investing in stocks, the thorough, disciplined application of an intelligent research process is the best way to avoid as many disasters as possible. Of course, some scoundrels will slip through the cracks, and that's okay; but, as with everything in life, doing your homework is critical to a positive outcome.

There are as many ways to research a company as there are to skin a cat. In fact, there are probably even more ways to research a company than there are to run a screen! However, the goal of every research process is the same: to assess the future return potential of an investment.

My research process is two-pronged: I simultaneously assess qualitative and quantitative aspects of the company along the way. While the process of researching each company feels unique to that company, the framework for my process—once

I have established that there is a real stated, philosophically supported and proven commitment to the dividend—is as follows.

STEP 1: ASSESS DIVIDEND SUSTAINABILITY

Qualitative

Management and board philosophy

The most important metric to consider when evaluating a dividend paying company is not the hard data, but rather the soft and subjective nature of the dividend. An investor absolutely must understand the company's commitment to paying a dividend and its philosophy surrounding why it pays dividends.

With the benefit of the search function, it is fairly easy to comb through previous earnings call transcripts and read exactly how the CEO or CFO addresses the dividend each quarter. You will find that the language surrounding the dividend varies greatly by company.

Take, for example, Dow Inc., which—following a fairly messy merger and breakup with DuPont—spun back off in 2019 as an independent entity. Upon the spinoff, Dow's businesses were huge cash flow generators but had limited growth potential. As the company emerged as its own entity, management used extremely strong language to explain that they knew that the bulk of shareholder return would come from a high—and achievable—dividend:

> We will ensure a leading dividend at spin. Our long-term dividend payout ratio target of 45% of net income is absolutely attractive relative to industry peers, and buybacks will play an important role. To that end, we intend to repurchase at least 20% of net income over the near-term. Our commitment to shareholder returns is a top priority of the Board and the Dow management team.

Then again, during the Covid-19 pandemic, when the world seemed dark and doomed, management reassured shareholders by saying in their Q1 2020 earnings call: "We remain committed to our dividend and are confident that we will be able to maintain it through this challenging time."

While Dow's use of language is precise, it is not uncommon for truly dedicated dividend payers to convey the same sentiment. It is also easy to follow the consistency of language between earnings calls. Importantly, if this is followed regularly, any shift in tone should usually be fairly obvious.

Dividend history

This is incredibly straightforward to assess, as the history of dividend payments is readily available. Currently, we investors have the rare gift of both recent and useful 20/20 hindsight. We can look back to the Great Financial Crisis of 2008/2009 and see if a company was able to maintain its dividend in a severe and prolonged economic downturn and bear market. Similarly, we can look at 2020 and see what happened during the extreme global economic shutdown that was triggered by the pandemic. While what we prefer to see is the maintenance of the dividend, it is also acceptable to see a suspension or reduction of the dividend followed by an immediate return to previous levels as soon as the crisis has passed.

History of financial discipline

Have leverage ratios remained consistent and as expected? Is there any history of overpaying for acquisitions?

Quantitative

Free cash flow

Unlike earnings, which can be impacted by non-cash items like depreciation and amortization, free cash flow is simply the cash that a company generates after it has paid for all of its operating and capital expenses. This "extra" cash can be used to pay dividends, buy back stock, hoarded for a rainy day or used to create more growth opportunities, either organically or through acquisitions. The questions a dividend income investor must ask themselves are: "Is the historical and projected free cash flow both significant and consistent? If not, why not? If so, what economic or industry factors could alter the consistency of the free cash flow in the future?"

Dividend coverage

Depending on the type of company, different metrics should be evaluated for dividend coverage. For ordinary common stocks, earnings are perfectly useful. For REITs, which have massive depreciation that distorts earnings, funds from operations are a better metric to determine if the business can generate sufficient cash to cover the dividend. For MLPs—whose earnings are skewed by the massive depreciation generated from their ownership of midstream energy assets, like oil and gas pipelines—the right metric to look at is cash available for distribution. We are simply seeking to answer the question: "Do the earnings/funds from operations/cash available for distribution exceed, with a reasonable cushion, the annual expected dividend?"

Balance sheet strength and leverage

Evaluating the debt ratios and the company's ability to pay off debts with ample short-term liquidity is critical to ensure it will be possible both to operate the business and to pay out dividends. However, the measures and levels of leverage vary between different types of companies. Understanding a reasonable level of leverage is tricky because an appropriate and manageable amount of leverage varies by company and industry. Real estate companies that have tenants with very long-term leases and extremely predictable future revenues appropriately carry high leverage levels. And why not? If a company knows it can borrow at 3% and earn an extremely low-risk, very long-term 7% on its investment, it really should borrow more.

On the other hand, companies with less visibility or more cyclicality to earnings—like Seagate, a high dividend paying technology company that manufactures hard disk drive memory—cannot afford to maintain such high leverage levels because of the cyclicality of their earnings streams.

Leverage should not be viewed as automatically good or bad, but rather assessed for appropriateness given the company's business, industry history and outlook.

Dividend growth

Like dividend history, past and future dividend growth is usually fairly easy to assess. The history is transparent: most companies either annually increase the dividend incrementally or maintain a steady dividend with occasional increases. A clear history of steady incremental increases is preferable to a flat dividend and makes future trends fairly easy to predict. Usually, companies that have a history of regular dividend increases will address future increases at least annually during their investor days or quarterly earnings calls.

STEP 2: EVALUATE EARNINGS AND DIVIDEND GROWTH POTENTIAL

Qualitative

Quality of the management and board of directors

Consistent earnings and dividend growth are highly reliant on a capable and effective management team, and assessing this may be the most difficult challenge in the entire investment process because it is so completely subjective. Most CEOs are born salespeople and can inspire confidence, with an uncanny ability to make even the most lackluster business sound compelling. While we can gain significant and useful insight from a management team's track record, the ubiquitous investment disclosure applies here too: past performance is not a guarantee of future returns.

Evaluating the board is critical too, and this should be done with a very shrewd and cynical eye. In John Carreyrou's book *Bad Blood*, he tells the story of the rise and fall of sham company Theranos. Led by the charismatic Elizabeth Holmes, it became the darling of Silicon Valley and attracted a veritable who's who to its board, including the likes of Henry Kissinger, James Mattis and George Shultz. A simple glance at board member résumés would leave anyone staggeringly impressed. However, what no board member had was biotech or hematology experience. When evaluating a board, it is critical to look deep into the bios and make sure that there is applicable experience, no nepotism and no sneaky placement of friends or patsies on the board. There should be serious people with relevant but broad experience, and enough diversity of perspective to lower the odds of toxic groupthink degenerating the effectiveness of the board's oversight.

Competitive position

While subjective, assessing a company's competitive position is frequently relatively straightforward. Think about AT&T versus Verizon versus T-Mobile: in an industry with only three real competitors, it's easy enough to look at the number of subscribers over the years and see how the market share is traded around. While T-Mobile has become the biggest winner of the three, both AT&T and Verizon still generate significant profits and, for the most part, maintain their relative market positions.

Alternatively, one can think about Bed Bath & Beyond versus Amazon. It was pretty obvious that a significant portion of what Bed Bath & Beyond was selling could easily be obtained elsewhere, either at the grocery store or online, and delivered for free in two days or less—both far preferable to driving to Bed Bath & Beyond, navigating its uncomfortable narrow aisles and waiting in the inexplicably long checkout lines.

With competitors like General Mills versus Kraft Heinz, Macy's versus Nordstrom and Intel versus AMD, the competitive positioning is significantly more difficult to assess and involves deeper digging and harder-to-access industry-specific data and knowledge.

Industry trends

Depending on how you look at it, this is where the research can get either fun or very intimidating! Each industry is unique and the companies within it are even more so.

At this moment in time, an unusual situation is developing in the fast-food industry. Novo Nordisk, a Danish pharmaceuticals company, has produced a drug for diabetes called Ozempic. However, it was discovered that Ozempic, through its use of GLP1 inhibitors, can also help with weight loss. To many, this is the holy grail that they've been looking for and sales of Ozempic have exploded. Fascinatingly, companies that sell and produce highly caloric food have seen their share prices come under significant pressure, as it is presumed that the high-calorie food industry will see revenue pressure as people consume fewer calories due to the proliferation of these new weight loss drugs. Wild, right? Indeed, Walmart recently put out a statement saying that it has seen a significant reduction in sales of high-calorie food.

When this trend hit, I was in the process of researching fast-food chain Wendy's. Understanding the reality of this new use of GLP1 drugs and their ability to suppress appetite added a whole new layer of complexity to the research process.

Whether this trend fizzles out or picks up steam is anyone's guess; but as a good analyst, one must look deeply into each industry and all its unique drivers and idiosyncrasies.

Macroeconomic environment

The macroeconomic environment must always be considered when making investment decisions. Thinking about things like how rising or falling interest rates may affect a company's balance sheet is critical. For example, if a recession appears to be on the horizon, how might that impact consumer spending? If the government has allocated funds to a large infrastructure bill, who are the beneficiaries?

There are thousands, if not tens of thousands, of macroeconomic data points—enough to freeze anyone in their tracks as they try to think through all the trends that may impact their investments.

However, in my view, simplification here is best and investors should focus on the basics by asking themselves questions like: "Is the environment that we are in likely to be supportive of earnings growth? Are central bank policies restrictive or supportive of growth? Are consumers healthy, as reflected by their savings, spending, employment and wage growth? How will the current interest rate environment likely affect borrowing and debt servicing?"

5: RESEARCHING DIVIDEND COMPANIES

Barriers to entry

There is a major difference between getting into the airline, auto manufacturing or semiconductor testing equipment business and getting into the clothing or makeup business.

Take Intel, for example. It is building a new semiconductor fabrication plant in Arizona to try to bring manufacturing back to the United States. That "fab" alone is likely to cost $25 billion! The barriers to entry are extremely high as, globally, only a handful of semiconductor companies have the operational expertise to manufacture chips at that cost and scale.

On the other hand, just about anyone can set up their own clothing store on Etsy or Shopify and compete, to some degree, with The Gap or American Eagle by selling the same products.

High or low barriers to entry are neither a qualifier nor a disqualifier; but they are a necessary consideration in the investment research process.

Quantitative

Earnings projections

There are two primary ways to predict earnings. One is to listen to what management is telling you and believe what they say. The other is to do extensive research on not just the company in question, but the industry overall to try to project what the future is most likely to hold.

Thankfully, for individual investors who have full-time jobs and/or a total lack of interest in spending 80 hours a week trying to discern a company's future earnings potential, the big investment banking firms and hundreds of boutique research firms have hordes of research analysts who dedicate their full time and attention to figuring this out. These analysts—while always imperfect and frequently incorrect—are, by and large, a smart, hardworking crew who do their best to project a company's financial future. Collectively, analyst projections can be useful and at least directionally accurate in predicting a company's future earnings potential.

In this wonderful age of ubiquitous information, anyone can find the consensus on future earnings expectations on the internet.

When buying dividend stocks, the thing to look for is that future earnings (or funds from operations, or cash available for distribution, or free cash flow) can sufficiently exceed the future expected dividends and show a future growth trajectory.

Balance sheet strength

This is of critical importance to the research process. When analyzing dividend companies, above all, try to ensure that future dividend payments are safe and likely to flow indefinitely to investors. The primary balance sheet items to look for are ample cash on hand and the structure of the debt.

Many companies that pay dividends tend to be mature, with very predictable revenues and earnings. As such, many are comfortable carrying debt and using the leverage that it can provide to increase overall earnings growth. Good companies structure this debt carefully, with a well-laddered portfolio of consistent debt maturities that were offered at times when interest rates were relatively low. It is critical to look at a company's debt maturity ladder and make sure that the cash on the balance sheet and future earnings will more than cover the maturing debt and interest payments.

STEP 3: RISK VERSUS RETURN ASSESSMENT

Qualitative

Earnings conviction

Gaining conviction about a company's future earnings is one of the hardest but most interesting parts of the investment process. To become convinced that earnings projections will be met, one must consider everything from management's track record of achieving stated goals to what the future could hold for an industry or product.

Recently, I read that Chinese electric car maker BYD can profitably produce electric vehicles (EVs) for under $10,000 and that automakers everywhere are panicking. If you were considering investing in Ford or Honda, for example, you might ask yourself if those management teams considered BYD producing $10,000 cars when issuing revenue and earnings guidance. Another good question to consider is if the profitability is real or if the Chinese government is subsidizing to create profitability as a form of economic warfare. And if so, does it matter? Will US, European and South Asian consumers buy $10,000 Chinese EVs; and if so, what portion of Ford's and Honda's sales could be disrupted? How reliable can earnings projections really be when, just yesterday, no one was even thinking about $10,000 EVs from China?

Worst-case scenario analysis

Particularly for a dividend portfolio, where many investors rely on the income stream to support their lifestyle, it is critical to think about what could go wrong. Often, this is made a little easier by the management teams of companies with high dividend yields, who stress test dividends for a variety of worst-case scenarios.

As terrible as they were at the time, the Great Financial Crisis and the Covid-19 pandemic make for excellent worst-case scenario testing. One can look back and see if, during those dark and disrupted periods, the earnings still covered the dividend and the company continued to pay dividends throughout the turmoil.

While it can be challenging and interesting (as well as paranoia-inducing), it is critical to consider what else might derail a dividend. For venerable companies like Nordstrom and Macy's, it was the shift to online shopping. For Ryman Properties and Six Flags, it was the cessation of entertainment travel and experiences during the pandemic. For many of the upstream and downstream energy companies that incorporated as MLPs in the early/mid-2000s, it was the plunge in oil prices in 2015/2016.

Hopefully, worst-case scenarios will not come to pass; but thinking through what could reduce earnings to the point that management would cut the dividend is a critical part of the process.

Management meetings

Once upon a time, private, in-person meetings with management teams were a critical part of the research process. Then, in the 2000s, two things happened. The first was a rash of insider trading cases that took down everyone from individuals like Martha Stewart to hedge funds like former behemoths Galleon and SAC. The second was a dramatic technological development that afforded instant, continuous and ubiquitous access to flawless recordings and transcripts of meetings.

Following the insider trading cases, management teams became even more cautious about disseminating any non-public information. In fact, this has gone so far that many company presentations feel almost entirely scripted, and CEOs, CFOs and investor relations teams are groomed to within an inch of their lives not to go even one syllable off-script. So, whether it is an earnings call, an industry conference or a small group meeting, the content of what is said will be nearly identical. Most investor questions receive canned answers that have been pre-approved and carefully scripted by compliance teams so that all investors in all forums receive the same information (which is a good thing for everyday investors).

The positive and wonderful side of why individual company meetings are not as necessary as they once were is the near-complete accessibility of company commentary. Almost any earnings call, investor day or research conference can be watched or listened to online. Some people like to tune out the bias of management's tone and for them, written transcripts are immediately accessible. At their leisure, from whatever location they wish to watch or read from, management's shareholder communications are readily available.

For me, it is critical to watch management meetings regularly to monitor for changes to language, tone and body language—both positive and negative.

I find that management meetings are useful when as much homework as possible has been done in advance, but one still needs a better understanding of the business and what could happen to the company or industry in various economic scenarios to complete the research process. Management meetings are useful for understanding trends and relationships, but are no longer useful for gleaning small bits of information that no one else has.

That said, I still value meeting with management teams as often as possible, because it helps me focus and really understand a business. However, for many successful investors, these types of meetings invite bias and noise, while numbers and facts provide all the information they need to make a smart investment decision.

Like so much in investing, the process itself matters less than the consistent and disciplined application of each investor's unique process.

Playing devil's advocate

For each investment, questions about what is being missed or misunderstood must be asked. To do this effectively, a mutually respectful and trusting relationship with an investment sparring partner is critical. It is hard to play the role of one's own devil's advocate because, as the researcher in the process, the depth of perspective naturally creates a bias and closeness to the potential investment that make it nearly impossible also to maintain an objective aloofness to the situation.

However, there is a Catch-22 here: as myriad uncertainties will be revealed—many of which will remain permanent uncertainties—one must be careful not to become frozen in place and rendered unable to invest.

Quantitative

Relative valuation

One of the simplest and most insightful metrics is the relative valuation of peers. The most common ratio is price to earnings; but often, enterprise value to earnings before interest, taxes, depreciation and amortization (EBITDA) is a more appropriate measure.

When looking at very similar companies, widely divergent valuations can serve as both a red flag and a signal of opportunity created by a mispricing.

Absolute valuation

Some companies or situations are so unique that using a peer reference point for valuation is worthless. Sometimes, a company is sufficiently distinctive that it needs to be considered on both an absolute basis and a relative basis.

When thinking about a company on an absolute valuation basis, one might ask: "Does this valuation multiple sound

5: RESEARCHING DIVIDEND COMPANIES

logical with respect to this specific company's future growth prospects?" For example, if a company has expected earnings growth of 6% and a 4% dividend yield, and trades at a price-to-earnings multiple of 9x, well, that combination seems reasonable and would point to a fairly valued stock price. Alternatively, where a company has 6% expected earnings growth, a 0.8% dividend yield and a 26x price-to-earnings multiple, that combination does not seem reasonable and would suggest an overvalued stock price.

US Supreme Court Justice Potter Steward once said: "It's hard to define pornography, but I know it when I see it" (not the actual quote, but the common paraphrase).

Determining an appropriate valuation on an absolute basis is similar. It's hard to define, but you know what is reasonable and unreasonable when you see it.

Yield versus peers

When looking at dividend stocks, this is an extremely informative measure of relative valuation and often provides insight into the management and board and their relationship with shareholders. The earlier example of United Rentals and H&E is a perfect illustration of two peer companies with different capital allocation objectives: create shareholder return through acquisition versus create shareholder return through return of cash.

However, in many cases, peer companies will have dividend yields that are closer to each other, like 3.5% and 4.5%. From there, tremendous insight can be gained by understanding why there is a difference. The research process should try to determine if the yield differential is a result of one company experiencing a greater stock return than the other or of one growing the dividend more than the other, and why.

Later in the book, when I discuss my failed investment in Advance Auto Parts (AAP), you will be able to see how the difference in yield versus peers put up a red flag to which I should have paid more attention.

Debt and leverage

Many of us have been conditioned to think that debt is a bad thing. In fairness, many people and many companies have gone bankrupt though the irresponsible use of debt. However, many more people and companies have borrowed responsibly and used the funds to create great things: homes for their families and new products and technologies that have greatly benefited society. In fact, I recently stumbled across a wonderful story about Mike Keiser, who developed the Bandon Dunes golf courses in Oregon. The source of his wealth was from a greeting card company that he started decades earlier. His family wanted him to go to business school, the prospect of which sounded terrible to him; so instead, he tried to think up a business that could be fun and

5: RESEARCHING DIVIDEND COMPANIES

interesting and ensure he didn't have to spend the next two years of his life sitting in sterile classrooms surrounded by business wannabes. He came up with the idea of greetings cards on recycled paper. To start the business, Keiser and his partner borrowed $10,000 from their families; they eventually sold the company for $250 million in 2005!

Many dividend-paying companies are very mature and generate extremely predictable cash flows that can easily cover debt payments. When looking at debt and leverage, the question to ask is: "Does the cost of debt encumber or enhance the company's ability to generate and grow its earnings?"

A common and easy measure of leverage is debt to EBITDA. For example, many real estate companies comfortably maintain leverage ratios of 4–5x. In other industries, this would seem excessive; but given the assurance and predictability of future rent collections, the debt can easily be serviced.

Another data point that I like to look at to be sure that a company can easily pay its bond investors is the interest coverage ratio. This is measured by dividing earnings before interest and taxes by the interest expense on all the company's debt.

Do not be scared off by the use of debt and leverage; but do take care to dig deep and understand the company's ability to handle the debt that it carries.

STEP 4: DECIDING WHETHER TO INVEST

Once thorough research has been conducted, data has been assimilated and future return potential has been assessed, it is time to decide if it makes sense to initiate a new position into the portfolio. This is where the idea of opportunity cost comes in and the following questions should be asked:

- "Is the new position likely to return more than any of the existing holdings?"
- "If the investment is going to be made in a taxable portfolio and cash is not available for the new investment, will the sale of an existing holding create such a big tax bill that the potential return advantage of the new security may not offset the tax bill incurred by the sale to generate cash for the new purchase?"
- "Will the new investment improve the overall yield *and* the overall return potential of the portfolio?"

After careful consideration, it is time to decide whether to invest or pass.

As the quote at the top of this chapter reminds us, avoiding disasters is extremely important. After a long and laborious research process, deciding to pass can be incredibly difficult because so much work has already been expended. Perhaps taking a pass is more palatable when it is framed as an active portfolio management decision and not just wasted effort.

5: RESEARCHING DIVIDEND COMPANIES

Avoiding a 30% loss is absolutely as useful to the portfolio as securing a 30% gain and only a thorough research process can help you make a well-considered investment decision either to buy or not to buy.

6
STRUCTURING A DIVIDEND STOCK PORTFOLIO

"Diversification may preserve wealth, but concentration builds wealth."

—*Warren Buffett*

SEVERAL years ago, during an appearance on CNBC, I had a rare and brief moment of (self-considered) brilliance. We had a celebrity guest on the show with us that day and he was asking us for advice on an endless laundry list of stocks that he had in his own, self-directed stock portfolio. It dawned on me that many individuals' portfolios are like their closets: storage units for dozens of dated, useless, squirreled-away pieces of clothing that no one in their right mind would still own, but for some detached-from-reality sentimentality. Maybe I had this epiphany because I have reviewed a few too many portfolios with dozens or hundreds of positions, many of meaningless size. Maybe I was projecting because my closet is, most certainly, guilty as charged.

For those of us with normal closet space, real estate is valuable and holding onto my 1990s Thomas Pink shirt really is completely ridiculous. So is holding on to 12 tiny stock positions, each totaling 0.25% of an investment portfolio, just because each one has out-of-date rationale and sentimental attachment. An investor would be much better off holding one well-researched, well-considered, meaningfully sized 3% position with reasonable upside potential.

A common mistake that I find many individuals and (sadly) professionals succumb to when choosing to invest rather than pass is FOMO: fear of missing out. It is critical to always remember that a good portfolio does not need to own every single good investment. In fact, by trying to own every single good investment, what often happens is that a portfolio becomes diluted with dozens, or even hundreds, of little positions. In a portfolio that is so diluted, even a huge winner has little overall impact. Of course, the reverse is true too: a huge loser also has relatively little impact.

History has shown that a relatively concentrated portfolio can offer a higher rate of relative performance investment success. Consider Warren Buffett, for example: he has long held a portfolio of between 40 and 50 companies and has enjoyed remarkable success. Some years he outpaces the broader markets, others he does not; but by religiously applying a thorough research process, he has avoided some disasters and allowed for compounding over the long term to take care of the rest.

The success potential of a reasonably concentrated portfolio has also been mathematically supported by Harry Markowitz's

6: STRUCTURING A DIVIDEND STOCK PORTFOLIO

work on modern portfolio theory (MPT). One of the most important concepts of MPT is the idea of appropriate diversification for an optimal portfolio. MPT can be used for asset allocation, but also to demonstrate that portfolios with over 50(ish) stocks no longer diversify away meaningful risk. In my experience, an optimally sized portfolio that provides meaningful risk diversification should be in the 30–50 stock range (see Figure 6.1). Coincidentally, this is a number that a good portfolio manager can reasonably expect to maintain through ongoing research and analysis.

Figure 6.1: Risk reduction through portfolio size by number of stocks

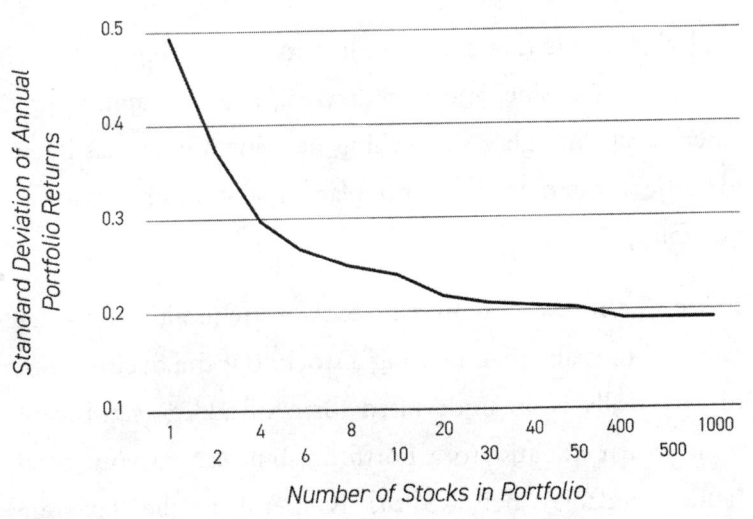

Source: Elton and Gruber.

So, if you believe this study to be a useful tool for thinking through position sizing and managing a focused portfolio of

30–50 stock positions, after the research process is complete and a new investment has been successfully identified, the question of opportunity cost arises.

Opportunity cost, defined as the value of what you may lose when deciding between two or more choices, is a critical assessment when considering whether to add any new investment to a portfolio. If the research process has been completed and a new investment candidate has been identified with upside potential of 15%, then each holding in the existing portfolio needs to be reviewed to see if it has more or less than 15% upside. And then, for taxable portfolios, the tax consequences must also be considered.

So, let's presume that every holding in the existing portfolio also has 15% upside, and that they each have a capital gain. Then, even though a compelling new investment has been identified, there really is no place for it in the existing portfolio.

It seems that not owning a stock is frequently a harder decision to make than owning a stock; but the decision not to buy really is an underrated form of adding significant total return not just to a portfolio, but also to your total (and spendable) net wealth. Remember, the tax due from realizing capital gains does not impact a portfolio's investment return, but it certainly does impact your personal balance sheet.

6: STRUCTURING A DIVIDEND STOCK PORTFOLIO

A frequently underappreciated, yet critically important, part of portfolio construction is position sizing. This is another area where there is no one correct answer. In my portfolios, most new positions start at about 3%. In rare cases, I may start at 2% with the expectation that I will add another 1% in the future.

When portfolio managers are interviewed by consultants who are looking to invest significant assets in their strategies, position sizing is usually an important topic of conversation. Early on in my career, I was interviewed by one such consultant and it felt like my simple "We usually start new positions at 3%" answer was flimsy. I went on to explain that sometimes if the company has a very small market capitalization and liquidity, and both the entry and exit to the position may be challenging, I might make it a 2% position. And similarly, if there is a mega-cap company where my conviction is enormous, I might start at 3.5%. From there, I will let the position size float, usually trimming it if it grows to over 5%. If a position size falls to 1%, I will either sell it because I have reassessed the investment thesis and determined it a failure or add to it because, while the share price is down, the investment thesis is intact.

Even with this bulked-up explanation, it seemed that my methodology was too unscientific and just felt weak once I looked at it through the consultant's eyes. So, I asked, "What do the really big managers who manage tens of billions of dollars do?" The consultant explained that there are dozens of studies on optimal position sizing, as well as complex mathematical optimization programs, each with a different theory or approach. They sound smart but are overly complicated and add little discernable value; so, he told me, essentially, what almost everyone else does is exactly what I do: choose a round number that will give each position a meaningful weight within the context of the portfolio that they are managing.

I know professional portfolio managers who manage equal-weighted portfolios of 100 stocks where each position starts at 1% and others who have only nine stocks that they hold for many years on end. What is most important is that the positions and their sizing are intentional. Having a portfolio that has accidentally become 20% weighted to a single company like Apple brings in more single-stock risk than most investors are really willing to accept. And while it may have worked out so far, over the years I have seen clients who had that kind of overexposure to companies like 3M, Lehman Brothers and General Electric (which, once upon a time, were thought of with as much confidence and love as Apple is today, because for decades they pretty much only went up) and who later were skunked when the businesses stumbled or even crumbled.

Equally inappropriate, but less dangerous, for a portfolio is a big smattering of tiny, sub-0.5% positions. They take up

6: STRUCTURING A DIVIDEND STOCK PORTFOLIO

too much mental energy and time to monitor and manage (remember—research is an ongoing process once you own a position), and are unlikely to move the needle on the overall portfolio.

The last thing to consider is whether you prefer to have a static or dynamic portfolio. This simply means that if you set something at 3%, does the weight always stay at 3% with regular rebalances to bump it up or down? Or is the portfolio dynamic, whereby the position sizes are allowed to move freely as the share prices change? At the individual level, this is an easy question to answer and most investors will choose to allow the portfolio to dynamically fluctuate, driven by share price volatility. For institutional portfolio managers that set a model and are constantly investing new client monies, the decision to run a static or dynamic model becomes more complex.

7

MANAGING DIVIDEND CUTS AND REDUCTIONS

"Your success in investing will depend in part on your character and guts and in part on your ability to realize, at the height of ebullience and the depth of despair alike, that this too shall pass."

—Jack Bogle

When constructing a portfolio with the aim of generating a stable, long-term dividend income stream, the prospect of a company cutting its dividend and interrupting that income stream may seem catastrophic. Realistically, however, in a portfolio of 30-plus stocks, on average, one of them will cut or trim its dividend each year. And yes, it stinks when it happens; but it is just a normal part of the investment process that needs to be managed and overcome.

The most constructive analogy that I have been able to come up with is that managing a portfolio of 30–50 stocks is like managing a business with 30–50 people. (Except a lot easier, because poor performers can be divested by simply entering a sell order and without any tears, emotion or threats of retaliation.) Inevitably, if you are managing a business—whether it is a retail store, an IT support team or a nursery school—someone is likely to quit or need to be fired each year. Losing an employee, when it happens, is the pits. Significant time and effort go into the hiring and training of each employee. Often, it takes months or even years before an employee becomes a truly useful and productive contributor to the larger enterprise. The same is true for stocks in a portfolio. Tremendous effort goes into the research: a new investment often involves tens or even hundreds of hours of reading, analysis, conversation, calculation and consideration. Losing one to a dividend cut is never optimal; but in a well-diversified portfolio, it is always surmountable.

Interviewing new candidates for a role and training new hires take a lot more work than if the person being replaced had stayed and done a good job; but that is also just how life goes. As a hiring manager, you must go through the process: begin the search for a new person, sort through applications, interview candidates and eventually make a hire. In the interim, others pick up the slack and the organization continues to move forward.

It is exactly the same when managing a dividend income portfolio. Instead of posting a job on LinkedIn and sorting through 2,000 resumes, you just go back to Chapters 4 and 5: run a screen (which you should have been doing continuously in any case), find some decent candidates, go through the research process, decide on a new investment and move on.

One way to ease the transition for when the inevitable happens is to keep an up-to-date list of companies that are well researched, so that if and when you need to make a replacement, the process time is minimized. As we discussed in Chapter 6, as frequently happens when researching companies, perfectly great companies are identified but not bought because, at the time, it seems like everything else in the portfolio has the same—or better—upside potential. Once a company cuts a dividend, the opportunity cost equation changes and a stock that had been forced to sit on the sidelines can be brought into the mix relatively quickly.

Maybe an appropriate analogy here is the Broadway understudy: the actor who can fill in for the lead at a moment's notice. They're selected and trained to step in when the person ahead of them catches a cold or sprains an ankle. Keeping a solid shortlist of potential investment candidates makes the process smoother and—most importantly in the case of a dividend income producing portfolio—can help maintain an uninterrupted dividend income stream.

One of the biggest challenges when a company cuts a dividend is that it creates a feeling of demoralization and betrayal. Quite possibly, the management team may have recently reassured shareholders about their commitment to the dividend. Sometimes, the company may have more than enough free cash to cover the dividend but choose to alter its capital allocation plans anyway, leaving dividend-oriented shareholders with the feeling of being forsaken. Again, managing emotions is one of the most difficult challenges to long-term success.

I often marvel at baseball pitchers, especially those pitching to a chorus of loud cheers and jeers. These guys can have 50,000 people staring at them and throw ball after ball, give up a few runs and keep going with what—outwardly at least—looks like complete cool and confidence. They seem like they have ice water in their veins and just keep at it, throwing pitch after pitch as the fever in the stadium intensifies with each weak ball and each hit. Then, out of nowhere, they'll throw a few strikes, a batter will pop out and the inning is over. The truly successful baseball pitchers clear their heads and start anew with each and every pitch, unburdened by all that came before. They cannot and do not let one iota of self-doubt into their consciousness; they simply follow the process that has brought them such professional success—clear your head, look to the catcher for instructions, trust their well-practiced mechanics, windup, throw. As a portfolio manager, it's important to channel the same "fresh start" and put the past in the past as a learning experience, but never allow it to derail confidence. As with the baseball pitchers, a strong stock selection process helps overcome the self-doubt that could otherwise set in after a few lousy pitches. In order to keep going, just like a pitcher

7: MANAGING DIVIDEND CUTS AND REDUCTIONS

has a process for each and every ball thrown, so too should a portfolio manager. In times of doubt, especially those caused by dividend cuts and trims, it is helpful to remember to just follow the disciplined process that has worked so successfully in the past.

On the subject of baseball, I will now throw you a curveball! What is often harder to manage than a dividend cut is a dividend reduction. As we have discussed, while dividends and dividend increases are signals of a company's excellent financial health and dividend cuts are usually signs of a company's distress, a dividend reduction is not always so black and white. In fairness, a reduction can usually be viewed the same as a cut—an indication that something is likely wrong.

However, as was the case recently with 3M, a long-time Dividend Aristocrat, a reduction can result from a strategic corporate shift. In recent years, 3M has been embattled by class action lawsuits over PFAS (forever chemicals) and ear protection failures. The management and board reached a point where the liabilities were largely known; and they also decided to streamline the business by spinning off their healthcare unit, Solventum, into a separate entity. With the spinoff of Solventum, the remaining 3M business was able to reduce its debt but also reduced a significant portion of its EBITDA. As a result, the management team made the difficult decision to reduce the dividend. In doing so, the company unlocked significant shareholder value and repositioned itself for growth.

In the case of a dividend reduction, the dividend income investor should be careful not to cut off their nose to spite their face and just sell the shares immediately. Occasionally, the capital appreciation potential in the share price can be significant when a dividend is reduced for appropriate reasons that are understood by the investment community. In other cases, it may prove sensible to ride out the overreaction from other annoyed dividend shareholders and wait for a more attractive exit point once emotions have cooled.

Once again, investing is not black or white, but nuanced and demanding of additional research, thought and contemplation before action is taken.

8
SELL DISCIPLINE

"The most contrarian thing of all is not to oppose the crowd but to think for yourself."

—*Peter Thiel*

A STRONG and consistent sell discipline is perhaps the most underappreciated attribute of an excellent investor. It is also frequently the most obvious thing that separates recreational and professional investors.

Professionally managed portfolios are often much more concentrated than self-managed individual portfolios. This is because professionals understand the value of position sizing and opportunity costs (Chapter 6); but they also have been trained to divorce emotion from the holding process and to view stocks as simply stocks—not love affairs.

My husband is an unfortunate lifelong avid Baltimore Orioles fan. I am always happy to go along to a game. I frequently am upset when he's angry that someone isn't pitching well and find it heartless when players are traded around. I see them as young kids trying their best, who deserve some time, love and a chance. John—as well as the team's owners and managers—

see them as objects in a portfolio with the sole objective of generating performance. If they cannot perform as they did when they were drafted or traded, they're removed from the lineup. Oddly, what I find heartless in baseball is obviously the correct strategy for managing a portfolio of stocks. (But then again, while you might have feelings about stocks, the stocks do not have feelings about you!)

For a dividend-focused portfolio, the following are optimal sell triggers.

THE STOCK REACHES A FULL VALUATION

Reaching a full valuation is the best possible outcome. It means that the share price has appreciated enough to close the gap between where you initially bought the shares and the price that you think they should be worth. Almost always, this also means that the dividend yield has now become a fraction of what it was when the shares were initially purchased.

We often talk about the slow and steady increasing nature of dividends and the volatile big moves of share prices. Usually, in a "full valuation" sale, the percentage increase in the share price has outpaced the percentage increase of the dividend.

An excellent example is my 2018 investment in large pharmaceutical company and Dividend Aristocrat Abbvie. When I initially purchased Abbvie, the dividend yield was about 5% and I believed that the capital appreciation potential over the coming years should be north of 20%. Happily, my expectations were exceeded and Abbvie's shares nearly doubled within a few years. This left the stock trading with a dividend yield of under 3.5% and a price-to-earnings multiple well in excess of its large pharmaceutical company peers. As part of an ongoing research process and constant opportunity cost assessment, I evaluated the further upside potential for Abbvie from that point forward. I assessed if the premium valuation suggested outsized earnings growth ahead or if the share price had become too rich for the realistic earnings growth. In this case, I concluded that it was the latter and exited the shares with a very nice profit.

You will note from Figure 8.1 that even though Abbvie increased its dividend significantly, the share price increase eclipsed the pace of the dividend increase, rendering the dividend yield much lower than it was at the time of the initial purchase.

Figure 8.1: Abbvie share price and dividend (DPS) growth (2018–2024)

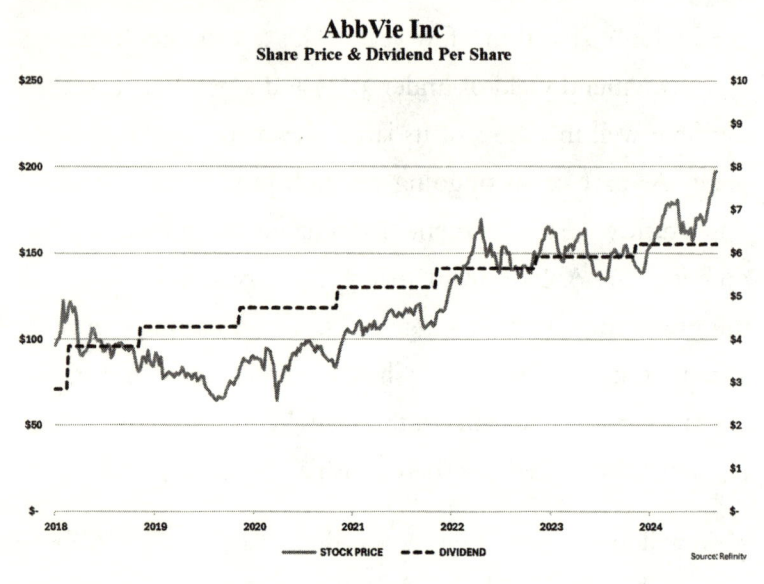

AbbVie Inc
Share Price & Dividend Per Share

[Chart showing stock price and dividend from 2018 to 2024, with stock price ranging from ~$50 to $200+ (left axis) and dividend from $0 to $8 (right axis). Source: Refinitv]

THE DIVIDEND IS CUT OR REDUCED/A DIVIDEND CUT OR REDUCTION IS ANTICIPATED

It is best to keep ahead of a dividend cut rather than waiting for it to happen and hoping for the best. Most of the time, when a company cuts the dividend, no matter how highly anticipated the event, the shares trade down significantly and are slow to recover—indeed, sometimes they never recover.

In Chapter 5, when we talked about management meetings, we mentioned that much of the value comes from staying on top of changes in language and tone. Management frequently will begin to signal a cut to the dividend a couple of quarters before it actually happens. As a regular listener to investor calls, one can discern changes in the language about how strongly a company supports the dividend or what capital allocation priorities will be going forward.

Dividend cuts can also be anticipated where there is a deterioration in earnings that increases the payout ratio to the point of obvious discomfort or even unsustainability.

In any case, when a dividend is reduced significantly or cut completely, it almost always results in a violation of the original investment thesis that renders the current investment irrelevant for a dividend income portfolio; so out of adherence to discipline, the shares should be sold.

CONCERNS ABOUT THE MANAGEMENT

For the most part, the management teams of public companies are a fairly straight-shooting crowd—salesmen and eternal optimists, yes, but not liars or charlatans. They are heavily monitored by layers of regulatory organizations, from the Securities and Exchange Commission and the Internal Revenue Service (IRS) at the federal level to dozens of state and industry-specific regulators.

Some managers are more talented than others. Some are truly inept and terrible, but few are intentionally shady and deceptive.

Different investors have different approaches to evaluating a management team. I, for one, like to see them in person as often as possible, as it helps me detect any concerning shifts in body language or tone. Others, like my partner Greg Stanek, prefer to read the transcripts of meetings, as they can discern more without the speaker's personality or theatrics creating an emotional bias.

Generally, though, the only way to identify concerns over management is to regularly observe them one way or another, so that when there are negative shifts in tone or language, you can pick up on these.

In all the sales that I've made over the years, concerns about management have not been the leading cause; but the most memorable sale I ever made for this reason was that of American Realty Capital Properties, which I came to own after it acquired CapLease, a company that I had originally invested in coming out of the Great Financial Crisis.

The initial investment in CapLease was driven by a combination of a compelling valuation, high dividend yield and superb leadership by CEO Paul McDowell, who was open, honest, available and pragmatic. A few years after my initial investment, in 2013, CapLease was bought by American Capital, a company that went on an M&A bender. Shortly after the merger, I went to see the new CEO present at an industry conference and was stunned by the hot mess that I witnessed—exhausted, twitchy and apparently under significant stress. To say that I was spooked would be an understatement and the shares were sold in short order. Having bitten off way more than it could chew, within a few years American Realty filed for bankruptcy.

Fun story, but extremely uncommon.

VIOLATION OF THE ORIGINAL INVESTMENT THESIS WITH NO REPLACEMENT INVESTMENT THESIS

Like a relationship, sometimes things just do not work out as anticipated. Sometimes the dividend falls apart; sometimes the growth potential never materializes; sometimes the company simply stagnates—the multiple expansion that seemed probable never happens. These are the hardest kinds of positions to give up on, because it often seems like just a little more time will allow for the investment thesis to play out.

Personally, recognizing and coming to terms with the violation of the original investment thesis is my Achilles' heel of being a disciplined seller. For me, one of my greatest "edges" as an investor is patience. However, this edge can also work against me when my original investment thesis is violated and I believe that all that is really needed is patience. I often think that with just a little more time and a few more quarterly reports, the pieces will come together, when in reality the business is fundamentally off track and the shares should be sold.

As in life, self-awareness is half the battle. I would give you an example of some of my losing investments due to an incorrect investment thesis, but the list is far too long!

PART 3

CASE STUDIES OF PEOPLE AND STOCKS

IN this section, I have changed all the names, locations and portfolio values, but the stories are real—at least as I recall them…

Mike Rowe—a wonderfully colorful and smart human, as well as the host of the television programs *Dirty Jobs* and *Deadliest Catch*—wrote a delightful book of short stories titled *That's The Way I Heard It*. Well, for this next section, let's just say, "That's the way I remember it." To the best of my recollection, these stories are accurate and, perhaps more importantly, exactly how I remember them. Let's hope that the subjects of my stories remember them the same way that I do!

9
BILL AND HIS DEMAND FOR INCOME, INCOME, INCOME!

"It's not how much money you make, but how much money you keep, how hard it works for you and how many generations you keep it for."

—*Robert Kiyosaki*

BACK in 2009-ish, I began working with a man who, to this day, remains one of my most cherished clients. He and I had met a few years earlier, in 2005, when he was first interviewing investment managers and his accountant suggested he meet with me. Unfortunately, though, he initially decided to engage a larger, name-brand firm to oversee his substantial wealth. Bill was in an interesting situation: he had worked hard his entire life and earned a great salary that afforded him and his family a pretty luxurious lifestyle. When I first met him, he and his business partners had just sold the company that they had started 30 years previously. While they all would receive substantial liquid wealth from the sale, the days of a large and reliable paycheck were over. He would need the money from the sale of his company to support the lifestyle to which he had become accustomed. (We're talking multiple homes, Range Rovers and Bentleys, but not private jets or yachts.)

Prior to 2005, Bill had never invested in the stock market. Most of the company's profits, besides the salaries that he and his partners drew, had been reinvested into building their business—and a good investment decision it was! I reconnected with Bill in 2007 when he was looking for a manager for his brother's portfolio; then, when he called me again about his personal accounts, it was 2008 and the stock market was imploding. The volatility of stock market returns was making Bill incredibly anxious: to him, the market tumult seemed to confirm his fear that stocks were too risky and unreliable to deliver the consistent income that he needed, financially and emotionally. Part of the reason for Bill's concern was that he had inadvertently stepped on not one, but two landmines when he hired the big firm to manage his money: he had made the all-too-common mistake of hiring yes-men salesmen posing as investment managers; and he had made strongly worded, poorly explained demands regarding how his money should be managed.

Bill is a large, handsome man who looks like an all-American college football player and has a very forceful and supremely confident nature—as many successful CEOs must. When he hired the large, name-brand firm, he essentially told them, "I WANT INCOME, I WANT INCOME, I WANT INCOME! MAXIMIZE MY

INCOME!" The investment firm, out of either ignorance or a bit of greed, gave Bill exactly what he wanted without explaining the risks to him—or probably understanding the risks themselves. The advisors did not pause to question why he was demanding income. The reason was that he was not yet comfortable with the fact that he no longer had a salary on which to depend. In addition, he had never invested before and had learned through his decades as a successful entrepreneur that cash flow is what matters most to the financial success of an enterprise. So, he demanded income, thinking that if income was pouring in, his investments must be working well for him and that he was in control of them.

The advisors never pushed back to explain that with dramatically outsized income comes outsized risk. They failed to ask him: "Do you really need that much income or would you be happier with less income, but from lower-risk instruments?"

When I saw Bill's portfolio in 2008, it was, quite simply, horrifying—loaded to the hilt with very high-yielding closed-end funds for his equity exposure and auction rate preferred securities in lieu of cash or money market funds. In and of itself, the structure of the closed-end funds was not the problem; the problem was that the funds that had been selected for Bill all utilized significant leverage to create well-above-average dividend yields. Making matters worse, each fund was essentially invested in the exact same things: utilities and real estate stocks. The concentration of the equity component of his portfolio was, frankly, unconscionable—even though it looked like a pile of different funds, it really was just leveraged REITs and utilities and nothing else.

Bill was then, and still is, a very sophisticated person: well read, well considered, well traveled and a shrewd businessman. He is not, however, a professional investor. So, when he saw a pile of funds that had 7%–9% yields and lots of different fund names, no red flags went up for him.

He did not know to ask: "How do they get the portfolio to yield 9% when the REITs and utilities that the fund is invested in only yield 4%–5%?" He did not know to ask: "Is my entire equity exposure really concentrated into two sectors?" And he did not know to ask: "What happens to closed-end funds when there is a severe market downturn?" The answers to those questions were: "Leverage, leverage, leverage." "Yes, your entire equity exposure is in two sectors." And lastly: "Panicked selling forces closed-end funds to sell holdings aggressively when the market is trading down, thus locking in your losses; and in closed-end funds that use leverage, this is severely compounded, frequently resulting in permanent loss of capital."

Bill began to consider looking for another manager in 2008 because he felt he wasn't getting clear, concise answers from the large asset manager. He did not know the exact

9: BILL AND HIS DEMAND FOR INCOME, INCOME, INCOME!

questions to ask, but he knew the answers he was getting were incoherent and misleading. For example, prior to 2008, auction rate preferred securities were a popular cash alternative. Almost everyone in the industry believed that they were equivalent to cash, but with higher yields and less liquidity (you had to wait seven, 14 or 28 days to sell at auction, but prior to the Great Financial Crisis they always traded at par). Bill's advisors piled him into these instruments to juice the income that he loved so much. They did not explain that these are not cash; nor did they explain that the auctions can fail and investors can find themselves without access to their cash (in their defense, I am certain that they did not know this—most people didn't, especially those who were really just salespeople and not thoughtful investors).

As the Great Financial Crisis wore on, Bill found that his portfolio with closed-end funds was down 60%–80% and had millions of dollars in auction rate preferred securities—which were supposed to be the same as cash—that he could not access for liquidity. The advisors that he had been working with gave him no straight answers. Again, in their defense, I'm sure they had even less idea about what was happening than he did—these folks were not that bright. When it became obvious that his "cash" was not indeed cash, Bill received no *mea culpas*, no apologies and still no straight answers as to what had happened or where things had gone wrong.

In 2013, four years after Bill moved his portfolio over to us, I did a post-mortem on the closed-end funds that he had previously held and found that less than half of them still existed. Most had been folded into other funds and sustained enormous permanent losses.

Simply demanding income without understanding how that income is generated can put an investor in very dicey territory.

Whether investing in an individual stock or a fund, it is essential that the sustainability of the income be easily explainable and easily understood. In my experience, every time the explanation for how investment income is generated has been convoluted or confusing, it has raised a red flag.

The investment business attracts greed and rewards sales. More times than not, advisors—despite having a few credential letters on their business cards—are salespeople and not professional, thoughtful investors. Most investors are compensated more highly for bringing in new business than for maintaining existing clients.

The investment advisory business preys on people who do not know how to ask the right questions—and this includes both clients and advisors alike. Over the years, I have learned that the ability to ask the right questions has little to do with intelligence and everything to do with having an investment management education. Often, this education is developed

9: BILL AND HIS DEMAND FOR INCOME, INCOME, INCOME!

over the course of decades through the natural course of investing a little here and a little there. In Bill's case, his low-level advisors who put him into products that superficially answered his demand for income themselves failed to ask pertinent questions about liquidity or the real risks of the securities they suggested for him. I think they genuinely had no idea how much risk his investments carried; yet I'm certain they knew exactly how much they made in commissions for selling him the wrong, risky products. His advisors also failed to ask why he was demanding income, or to then consider what would serve him best in the long term. Bill lost a significant amount of money because his low-level advisors weren't trained to think (perhaps intentionally) more deeply or ask meaningful questions about what he was asking for or what they were selling him. Bill, at that point in his investing career, simply had not yet built up the knowledge to ask the right questions.

The lesson from this story is that if you want or need income, it is critical to understand how that income is being generated and how it will be sustained through major market downturns. If the answer is not easily understandable, recognize it for the red flag that it is.

Oh, and one last fun story that I cannot resist sharing when it comes to Bill: each month, Bill has a disbursement from his investment account into his checking account to cover his living expenses. Initially, this money was sent via wire transfer and the custodian on the investment portfolio side would waive the $15 wire fee. His bank, however, repeatedly failed to waive the fee and it drove him nuts. For a control freak like Bill, wiring funds was the preferred transfer mechanism because it was done on the same day. One day, Bill decided he had had it with the $15 per transaction fee and asked if there was another way to transfer the funds. I explained that the money could be sent via an electronic funds transfer (EFT), which was free but took overnight to process; but I was worried that a 15-hour lag between the money leaving his investment account and being deposited into his checking account would make him uncomfortable. His response was: "Jenny, let me tell you something—I didn't get this rich wasting $180 a year on anything. Switch it to the EFT."

10
NATIONAL PROPERTIES TRUST

"You're not going to get very far in life based on what you already know. You're going to advance in life by what you're going to learn … So you gotta keep learning. And the thing about learning is, when you do it, you get to do it again and again and again. And the amount you know compared to the things that are knowable is always tiny. And if you think … memorizing a bunch of stuff is all there is to it, you'll find you're a one-legged man in an ass-kicking contest."

—*Charlie Munger*

INVESTMENT research conferences are wonderful forums for learning. At a conference, I can focus and dive deep into an industry or sector. Investors are afforded not only a front-row seat to how individual companies are thinking and operating, but frequently a robust view of both the industry under study and the market as a whole.

One of the very best parts about these events is hearing the questions that other portfolio managers and analysts are asking. Many times, I have gone to a conference with a lack of clarity about the market's direction or where there may be areas of opportunity and come away with crystal-clear thoughts on other subjects that were only tangentially related to the conference itself. Going to a research conference allows time for deep, contemplative thoughts that may otherwise be drowned out by the hullabaloo of everyday routines.

Back in 2010, I flew out to Chicago for the annual National Association of Real Estate Investment Trusts conference—an event that I have attended pretty much consistently for the past 25 years (although pandemics and babies might have sidetracked me occasionally!). Usually, the conference is held in New York, so going to Chicago was a nuisance—especially with a baby and a toddler at home. Thankfully, however, the effort was more than well rewarded.

Each year, dozens and dozens of commercial real estate companies are given 30 minutes apiece to present their business to a room full of investors. The two main days are intense and packed with insights. Participating companies range from billboard owners to metropolitan office building developers and everything in between. As you may recall from our discussion of Realty Income Trust in Chapter 3, one type of company within publicly traded commercial real estate that tends to work particularly well for dividend income strategies is the triple-net lease company. These companies own buildings that are then leased to tenants on a triple-net lease basis—which means that the tenant pays

10: NATIONAL PROPERTIES TRUST

for taxes, utilities and improvements. Due to the nature of the tenant's business—they are frequently big box stores, convenience stores or gas stations—the leases are often very long: 20 years or more. There is little variability in the future rents that the landlord will collect, as all of the expenses are covered by the tenant and the rental contract has escalators built in from the beginning. The downside is that significant growth is limited—it is a business that generates extremely consistent cash flows, operates with extremely high tenant occupancy and generally subscribes to a "slow and steady wins the race" philosophy.

At this particular conference, I was frustrated because the organizers had booked many of the triple-net lease companies in the same time slot, but in different rooms. At the time, I owned CapLease (the company discussed in Chapter 8 that sold to American Capital) and needed to go see them. I had also wanted to see National Retail Properties, but they were presenting at the same time, so I figured that I would just read the transcript later.

As the conference ended and attendees lined up for taxis, the hotel staff started organizing people going to the same locations to share rides. I got into my taxi with an impeccably dressed man whom I did not know. He wore a fancy suit, with the bottom buttons of the sleeves left unbuttoned to signal it was custom made—a big thing on Wall Street at the time (today, even off-the-rack suit jackets have real buttons that can be unbuttoned, so much of the cachet has been lost)—and he had an erudite South African accent. Knowing that we were stuck together for an hour, I struck up a conversation and asked him if he had enjoyed the conference.

As it turned out—and much to my great fortune—my cab-mate was Craig McNab, the CEO of National Retail Properties. I wound up getting a one-on-one, hour-long meeting with the CEO of the company I had most wanted to see!

There is a famous Maya Angelou quote that says: "I've learned that people will forget what you said, people will forget what you did, but people will never forget how you made them feel." I do not remember exactly how he phrased it, but as we spoke, I realized that my mission for my clients was identical to Craig's mission for his shareholders: create a stream of cash flow that is entirely reliable throughout any economic environment and that grows consistently over time. After returning to the office and conducting a thorough research process, I invested in National Retail Properties in 2010 and held it for nine years until I was forced to sell when the shares became flagrantly overvalued in 2019. Thankfully, following the pandemic, I was able to buy it back at a fair price.

The company has gone from owing 1,195 buildings in 2010 to 3,548 buildings in August 2024. Its earnings have grown steadily along the way—as has the hefty and consistent

10: NATIONAL PROPERTIES TRUST

dividend that it pays out to shareholders. While the share price has never been on a rocket-ship ride to the moon like some of the lovingly dubbed "Magnificent 7" (Microsoft, Apple, Amazon, Google, Nvidia, Meta and Tesla), it has provided shareholders with an excellent source of dependable return from both income and capital appreciation. Throughout even the worst of the Covid-19 pandemic, National Retail Properties' occupancy rates remained in the very high 90% range and the company's communications to shareholders were superb and comforting.

Oh, and one fun story that did not technically impact my decision to buy the stock, but certainly added confidence that we were in good hands: amid heavy traffic, as the taxi ride to O'Hare Airport wore on, the conversation naturally turned personal. Craig told me that today was a great day for the McNab family. Now, I hope that he forgives me for oversharing and for not being quite precise on the details here—after all, it was a long time ago! But as I recall the conversation, I asked him why and he said that it was the first day of his son's first real job. I asked him what his son would be doing. Given his fancy suit, fancy accent, fancy CEO job title and all, I presumed that he had hooked his son up with an internship with one of his fancy hedge fund friends from a fancy Ivy League school. Shame on me and my presumptions. He proudly told me that his son would be digging ditches for Florida Power and Light in South Florida for the summer. Now *that* was a work ethic I could respect!

Craig McNab led National Retail until 2017, when he turned the reins over to Jay Whitehurst. The transition was seamless and professional, and the company never missed a beat.

In the era of mega-personality CEOs and botched, ego-driven CEO transitions (I'm looking at you, Disney), the professionalism and seamlessness of this leadership transfer further underlined the quiet value of this company: delivering drama-free cash flow to shareholders.

Figure 10.1 shows the National Retail Properties share price and dividend for a 30-year period. This is a lovely depiction of a dividend stream that grows steadily despite a stock price that, over the short term, vacillates based on the stock market's vagaries.

Figure 10.1: National Retail Properties REIT share price and dividend (DPS) growth (1994–2023)

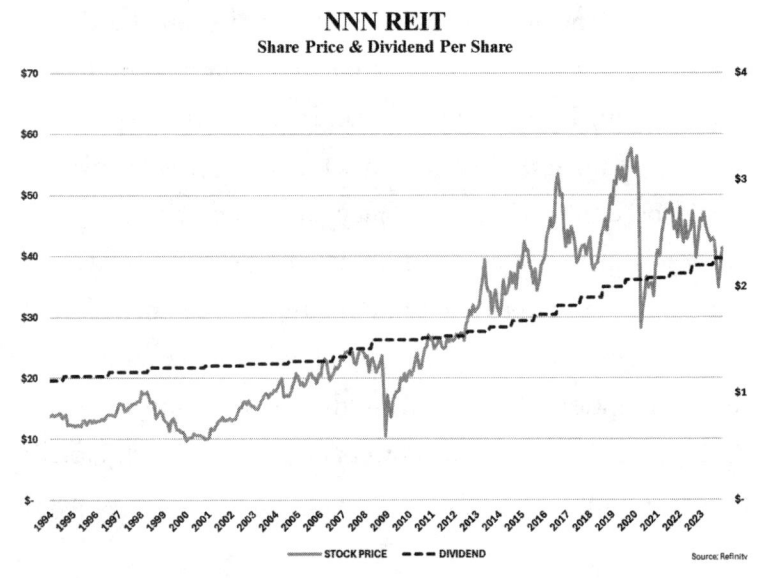

11

CAROL TOLD HER BROKER, "I CANNOT LOSE MONEY!"

"The biggest risk of all is not taking one."
—*Mellody Hobson*

IN 2011, a beloved friend of mine referred a woman that she knew socially to Gilman Hill. As it turned out, Carol had a wild story. She was widowed at a very young age when her dashing, daredevil husband died in a tragic alpine skiing accident, leaving her with two little kids and the weight of the world on her shoulders. The stress triggered a nearly paralyzing autoimmune disease that would have devastated any other mortal human. Thankfully, Carol—who has a superhuman positive spirit and a strong belief in God—tackled life's challenges head on. She moved her family from the cold of Idaho to Florida, which had a better climate for her condition. When she arrived in Florida, her savings were essentially at zero and she began selling real estate because it was a job with enough flexibility to allow her to still be a good mom to her two children, who had just lost their dad and moved thousands of miles away from home. It was also a job that could adapt around the multiple surgeries and health complications that she endured for decades.

Over the years, by living frugally and squirreling away as much as she could with every decent sale she made, Carol amassed an extremely respectable nest egg. For the sake of illustrative ease, we'll call it $1.5 million. When we first met, Carol was hoping to retire in about five years. (Spoiler alert: she is still working, just a little bit, because she just can't help herself.) I asked Carol: "How much a year do you need to live on?" She answered: "$100,000–$125,000 per year."

Conventional wisdom—and investment math—suggest that if you take 5% out of your portfolio each year, the portfolio should still be able to grow into the future and keep generating enough to support decades of future 5% withdrawals. The math is simple: historically, the stock market has grown at 8%–10% a year. If, on average, you take meaningfully less than the growth rate, your portfolio will be able to cover tax bills and management fees and still continue to grow and generate future returns.

When I initally reviewed Carol's portfolio, I was shocked to see that it was 100% invested in government bonds and Treasury inflation-protected securities. The yield-to-maturity on all of her investments was, to the best of my recollection, around 3%. Furthermore, as fixed-income vehicles that were intended to be held until they matured, the best return she would get would be the yield-to-maturity and no additional growth.

11: CAROL TOLD HER BROKER, "I CANNOT LOSE MONEY!"

I asked Carol why the portfolio was structured this way and if it was her idea or her broker's. Despite being a shrewd real estate agent and an extremely sophisticated person, Carol was not a sophisticated investor. She said that she did not really know why, but she had always told her broker: "I have worked way too hard for this money. It's all I have and I cannot afford to lose any of it."

Rather than doing their job and asking questions to understand the bigger picture, Carol's long-term needs or even why she believed that she could not lose money, the broker just said, "Okay" and put Carol's money into government bonds.

As I began to understand Carol and learn more about her portfolio and the history of how it had been invested, I was appalled by what I discovered. The amount of money that had been left on the table by not investing, even just partially, in stocks over the previous decades bordered on criminal (albeit not legally criminal—just very unethical).

I explained to Carol that if she were to spend $100,000 a year from her account ($100,000 of withdrawals on $1.5 million is a 6.7% draw rate) and it was only growing by about 3%, she would most likely deplete her account before the end of her life. Even if she did not want to lose money, she had to take some risk in her portfolio so that it could grow to a level to support $100,000 a year of spending—in other words, we needed the portfolio to grow by 33% to get from $1.5 million to $2 million. With $2 million invested in stocks, her portfolio should generate a significantly higher long-term return than it would with the bonds that she currently held, and she could actually get somewhere toward a functional retirement with her investments.

Carol is smart and pragmatic. Although it made her stomach turn, she agreed that by not taking any risk, she was in fact exposing her long-term financial health to massive risk: the risk of running out of money in her retirement. In April 2011, I got started with moving her out of her absolutely steady bonds and into stocks.

Naturally, in August 2011, the United States received a debt downgrade and by October the S&P 500 had plunged by 21%. Carol's stocks fell along with the market and to say that her confidence was rattled would be an understatement. I remember sitting on the porch while on vacation, speaking as quietly as I could so that I didn't wake up my napping kids, calling Carol to talk her down off the ledge.

As a real estate agent, and with the sage guidance of the mutual friend who had introduced us, Carol easily made the connection between real estate and dividend stocks. I explained to her that it was like she had just rented out a house to a new tenant with an extremely secure job—in fact, her tenant's Fortune 500 employer was paying her rent for the next five years, so there would be no risk of missing any rent payments. BUT a house down the block just sold at a crummy price for all sorts of unrelated reasons, which

11: CAROL TOLD HER BROKER, "I CANNOT LOSE MONEY!"

impacted the price of all the other houses on the block. It wasn't a question of if something had just gone terribly wrong, but rather of how long it would take before the house would be repriced to its previous level; and in the meantime, she would be collecting a safe and secure stream of rental income.

This made sense to Carol, and she gritted her teeth and got through it. Fast forward to today and her portfolio is producing nearly double the annual income that she had originally hoped for; and although she is still working, it's not at the same pace that she used to. She started taking money from the portfolio in 2019 to offset her reduced income.

The most important part of this story is the reminder that by not taking sensible risk in her portfolio, Carol introduced significant risk into her life. The second most important part is the analogy to real estate. We all know that the sale of a nearby house can impact the price of your house; but because most people are not immediately planning to sell their house, they do not care and it does not matter. Oftentimes, the same is true for stocks and the nanosecond-by-nanosecond share price fluctuations should never be equated with actual changes to the underlying value of a company.

During the editing of this book, out of the blue, Carol sent me the following email:

Jenny, did I ever tell you how much I appreciate you? If so, I am telling you again how much I appreciate you! Thank you for investing wisely and keeping me updated on the market. You certainly have achieved something amazing. It would have looked very different if I had stayed on the track I was on. It would have looked ugly. With love and gratitude…

To say this made my day (month, year, professional life…) would be an understatement! This is why I love dividend investing—it actually helps people live their lives.

12
H&R BLOCK

"The time to buy is when there's blood in the streets."
—*Baron Rothschild (apocryphal)*

THE Covid-19 pandemic created dramatic business distortions that disrupted and confused business leaders and investors alike. However, using history as a guide, one can easily see that incredible investment opportunities are often generated when fear and misunderstanding irrationally dislocate stock prices from the realistic value of the underlying company.

Take, for example, H&R Block, a company that seemingly everyone knows. H&R Block helps people file tax returns. Once you start to look around, it seems like every small town in America has a H&R Block location in a strip mall. In addition to its physical offices, H&R Block has an enormous internet-based tax return service. The business is fairly one-note and the revenues are extremely lumpy, as most people worry about filing tax returns between January and April. As you may recall, during the height of the pandemic, the US government extended tax filing deadlines and removed penalties for not filing taxes in 2020. As a result, H&R Block's revenue prospects became extremely uncertain. What had historically been a predictable business, with revenues generated as people either trotted into stores for help or logged in and used its software, became wildly disrupted.

The share price of H&R Block plunged from $25 per share just before the pandemic to a low of about $11 per share when the tax filing extensions were announced and investors realized that H&R Block's 2020 revenues and earnings would be dramatically impacted. Precisely what that impact would be was entirely unclear; and when the outlook is unclear, routinely—and particularly during market crises—investors freak out and assume a worst-case scenario. In this case, the plunge in share price seemed to be suggesting that investors believed that H&R Block would never file another tax return.

Admittedly, March through June 2020 was a particularly terrifying time in the world, when life as we all knew it became entirely disrupted. It felt like it might last forever—and it was scary. However, as the old adage says, the only two things in life that are guaranteed are death and taxes. To have assumed that people would stop both paying taxes *and* needing help in doing so was unrealistic at best and idiotic at worst. In the words of Warren Buffett: "The stock market is a device for transferring money from the impatient to the patient." As impatient, impulsive people sold their shares, I worked through my methodical research process and concluded that although it seemed like life was changing forever, it was not; and that H&R Block had a sufficiently strong balance sheet to weather an extreme dislocation in its revenue stream.

As the pandemic distortions subsided and life started resuming its normal trajectory, H&R Block's shares were slow to recover, even as its revenues headed toward all-time highs. I finally made my investment at about $20 per share in March 2021, when the dividend was around 5% and the shares were trading at a multiple of just 8x forward P/E—well under their historic multiple of 12x. I believed that as revenues and earnings returned to pre-pandemic levels, investors would take note and the shares would increase as the valuation multiple also expanded to a pre-pandemic multiple. My investment thesis proved accurate and strict adherence to sell discipline compelled me to divest the shares just a year later when they were trading at about $33 a share, the dividend was 3% and the multiple had expanded to 10x. With a yield of just 3% and limited potential for further upside, I thought that the funds from the sale of H&R Block would be better repurposed into a new investment with a higher yield and greater upside potential.

On the one hand, a 50%+ return in a year was a huge success. On the other hand, sometimes a strict sell discipline can limit the realization of further upside. When I made the decision to sell, I viewed H&R Block as a little more than fairly valued compared to its historic multiples and did not foresee such significant future earnings growth that the shares would trade for much more than where they were then priced.

At the time of writing this chapter, approximately two years after selling the shares, the stock now trades at $48 per share and has a yield of just 2.6%! So, while I made over 50% on the investment, I also left another 45% of return on the table. I did not anticipate that following the pandemic, H&R Block would sustain what appeared to be a permanently higher level of revenues and earnings. My expectation was for a return to pre-pandemic levels; not that 2021's revenues—which were driven by the complication of filing later, as well as reporting government subsidies—would become a new sustainable level of revenue. I also worried that H&R Block would be under constant margin pressure as tax filing increasingly moved to more efficient online channels. While this has clearly happened, the company has been able to sustain margins and drive earnings well beyond my expectations.

H&R Block has also consistently grown its dividends each year. That growth, however, has not been high enough to maintain a sufficiently large dividend yield to make the company eligible for the type of portfolio that I manage.

12: H&R BLOCK

Many times, a strong sell discipline helps identify stocks that need to be sold because continued ownership results in a negative opportunity cost as it takes up the spot of a better investment. Sometimes, the shares are overvalued and decline after they are sold (this is clearly the most satisfying outcome!). Other times, the shares continue to go up and up—and in the wake of their relentless rise, you are tormented for years!

13

LARRY AND LORI AND THE OUTER BANKS RENTAL PROPERTY

"Buy land, they're not making it anymore."

—*Mark Twain*

WHEN I started to write this chapter, I searched high and low for a great quote about the pitfalls of investing in real estate and could find none. It was all just line upon line from ivory tower billionaires about the virtues of owning land and getting rich. There were quotes about earning in your sleep and building monopolies, but none about late-night calls from tenants or vacation days and weekends spent on backbreaking property maintenance.

The following is the story of Larry and Lori; but there have also been stories from other clients over the years with rental properties in Orlando who had midnight calls about stoves infested with palmetto bugs and scandals at apartment complexes that were so bad they made the national news. Some clients owned houses in developments where the homeowners' association fees were so steep and the demands for upgrades to things like terracotta roof tiles so rigid that any future profit on the home was diminished by the cost of upkeep. Sometimes, town ordinances changed to disallow Airbnb rentals. There have been broken heating, ventilation and air conditioning systems and broken pipes—all requiring big account withdrawals. For all of my clients who own income-producing real estate, either it is more work than they anticipated or there is a property manager involved and then it is less profitable than initially anticipated.

Okay—now that you know where this is headed, on to Larry and Lori's story. Larry was a partner at a global industrial company that had a mandated retirement age of 60 (yes—a weirdly young age to force retirement). Upon his retirement, his ownership shares were cashed in and, after tax, he received $8 million. Larry and his wife, Lori, had always dreamed of owning a house in the Outer Banks of North Carolina and decided to split the cash in two: about half would be invested with Gilman Hill to produce dividend income to support their lifestyle when they needed it, while the remainder would be used to buy their Outer Banks dream home.

For those of you who are not familiar with the Outer Banks, it is a gorgeous, 200-mile-long stretch of barrier island primarily along the North Carolina coast. Most of the fancy homes have pools nestled into the dunes and long paths down to the stunning ocean beaches. When Larry and Lori bought their house, it was their expectation that the rental profit would be about $180,000–$200,000 per year.

13: LARRY AND LORI AND THE OUTER BANKS RENTAL PROPERTY

What they did not account for was the truism in the Mark Twain quote at the start of this chapter. Not only is land not being made anymore, but in many places, it is being eroded. Over the 15 years that they have owned the house, storms have damaged the coastline so severely that the bottom of the pool has been fully exposed. Over lunch, Larry would show me pictures of giant barges off the coast behind their house. These barges would pump sand from the ocean floor and then spray it back toward their house in order to fill in the missing ground around their pool and rebuild the beach that had been depleted from hundreds of feet wide to virtually nothing. The pictures were incredible.

The cost of repair and taxes to fund the beach replenishment wiped out many years of profits and then some. Washers and dryers would break during client stays and they would need to scramble around to get their property manager to deal with it. It felt like 100 things broke over the years, requiring enormous withdrawals from their investment account—because the rental income never did seem to cover the expenses of the house.

Over the nearly 15 years that I have managed Larry and Lori's investment portfolio, the S&P 500 returned about 14%. Their account—which was diversified between growth stocks, bonds, international stocks and, of course, dividend income stocks—produced a more meager return of about 9%. Despite significant cash withdrawals over the years, the value of their investment account is nearly 50% higher than the original net investment. Their house in the Outer Banks, for which they paid $3.2 million, has a Zillow estimate of around $5 million (for a compounded annual return of 3.0%). On balance, it has been a major source of stress, from what I can tell, costing more than it ever produced. Yes, there were some nice family vacations spent there—so, from an enjoyment perspective, it did have value. But from an investment perspective, it was a lot of work and produced not a huge amount.

To give you a mathematical perspective, the "net investment" in the portfolio was approximately $4.8 million. This means that all of the money that Larry and Lori ever contributed into the investment account was $4.8 million. Over the years, they have withdrawn and spent $3.4 million—and yet today, the total portfolio value is about $7.2 million! Despite all the withdrawals, the portfolio continues to generate over $340,000 per year of income—most of which is tax advantaged at a favorable dividend tax rate of just 15%.

Here we sit, 14 years later and the house is likely to be sold. The work is too much; the income is too low. However, the investment portfolio (which no longer has a fixed-income allocation) has caused Larry and Lori almost no stress over the years. Even during the worst of the pandemic and the 20% pullback in the Fall of 2018, the passive income that the stocks were generating was secure. The knowledge that the income was secure helped Larry and Lori get through the pullbacks along the way and encouraged their good investment behavior.

Historically, the market generates a positive return in three out of four years, yet on average declines by over 10% at some point in any given year. The most important part of having a successful investment portfolio is not to get rattled along the way and cash out at the market peaks or bottoms. If I am being totally honest about Larry and Lori, Larry wasn't always the easiest to keep invested over the years. His job had had a macroeconomic and geopolitical focus, and he viewed the world as a dark and troubled place that frequently scared the daylights out of him. Lori came from a family that had been to hell and back and ended up okay, so she viewed the world through a more resilient lens.

The knowledge that if Larry let his fear demons get the best of him, not only would their dividend income cease, but Lori would probably kill him if he cashed out at a low and wrecked their investment portfolio kept them invested and allowed them to ride out the lows and ultimately enjoy the long-term positive trend of investing in dividend income stocks.

14

ENTERPRISE PRODUCTS PARTNERS L.P.

"Compound interest is the eighth wonder of the world. He who understands it, earns it. He who doesn't, pays it."
—*Albert Einstein*

THE longest-serving (or surviving) investment in my dividend income portfolio is Enterprise Products Partners. Enterprise was originally formed in 1968 as a wholesale marketer of natural gas liquids. Over the years, as oil and gas exploration expanded, the company built up a network of pipelines, storage facilities and docks to help transport oil and gas around the United States. Today, Enterprise owns over 50,000 miles of pipelines, storage facilities for over 260 million barrels of liquid fossil fuel, 20 deepwater docks and 25 fractionation facilities.

Enterprise is a midstream energy company. "Midstream" refers to the transportation of fossil fuels between the "upstream" sector—which involves the exploration and production of fossil fuels—and the "downstream" sector, which involves the refining of fossil fuels and their distribution to end consumers. Many midstream companies have organized themselves as MLPs—a corporate structure that allows a tax-advantaged way to pay out free cash flow to shareholders. (The roots of this structure go back to 1981, when the US government wanted to encourage private companies to build out an energy infrastructure system across the United States.)

Back in the early 2000s, when I worked at Neuberger Berman, we had the incredible privilege of company CEOs and CFOs trotting through our office on a near-daily basis. At the time, only a few MLPs had gone public and the CEOs were happy to visit our offices as they sought to share their stories in the hope of enticing new investors to the industry.

While I do not remember the specific details of my first meeting with Enterprise—or peers like Magellan Midstream, Teppco Partners and Kinder Morgan—I vividly recall understanding what the businesses promised to investors: a very reliable and growing cash distribution stream. I recognized that their corporate strategy was directly aligned with my portfolio strategy: to create consistent and growing cash flows that could consistently be paid out to investors while successfully weathering any economic environment.

Back then, the midstream energy businesses were straightforward—the companies owned pipelines and the upstream producers would essentially rent space in those pipelines in order to transport their products out of the basins to wherever they needed to go next. At the time, that was mostly oil; whereas today, pipelines are dominated

14: ENTERPRISE PRODUCTS PARTNERS L.P.

by natural gas transportation. Companies like Chevron and Exxon rented the use of these pipelines and paid Enterprise and their peers a "toll" for their usage. Even though they were in the energy business, there was little to no commodity price risk to the MLPs. The sales pitch to investors was to think of them as "toll roads" for the transportation of fossil fuels; and in the early days, this was true. (Later, the space was flooded with loads of companies that were technically in the midstream energy space but did not have the same stable pipeline assets with the ability to create reliable, consistent cash flows with little to no commodity price correlation. In addition, many grew and diversified their businesses into other areas of the midstream energy market that often involved direct exposure to commodity prices.)

I initially invested in Enterprise in the early 2000s and still own it in client portfolios today. Looking at a stock chart reveals that at times, the shares have been on some wild rollercoaster rides. In the years following the Great Financial Crisis, a perfect storm of events led to a boom in investment in the midstream energy space. Interest rates and bond yields were low, energy prices were high and rising, and investors were skittish coming out of the crisis and looked toward companies and industries that were faring well. Both public and private equity dollars flooded into the space. New companies were created hand over fist and midstream energy funds of all types exploded. To juice the dividend yields, many of the funds used leverage. Salespeople from many of the biggest investment firms hocked the initial public offerings and newly created funds like a beer vendor at a ballpark. They failed, or intentionally neglected, to explain to investors that many of the new companies had significant revenue exposure to commodity prices; and they failed to explain the leverage or double taxation problems found in many of the funds.

Throughout the decades, Enterprise has thrived and survived by never straying from its disciplined goal of being an integral midstream energy company. Enterprise's long-term price and dividend charts can almost serve as a Rorschach test where different people will see different things. One perspective is: "Wow, that share price was up to $40 and still hasn't recovered. What a rollercoaster!" And another—coincidentally mine—is: "Wow, tuning out the noise of the industry-related mania and ensuing dislocation, that is a seriously steady long-term compounder. The compounding of dividends alone would have generated enormous wealth creation, but the share price has added capital appreciation over time too."

For a real dividend income investor—the person who wants their portfolio to provide the utility of delivering income through thick and thin—companies like Enterprise have been the rare stock that has made it easy to remain invested in over the course of multiple decades.

Figure 14.1: Enterprise Products Partners share price and dividend (2011–2024)

Enterprise Products Partners LP
Share Price & Dividend Per Share

STOCK PRICE — — — DIVIDEND

Source: Refinitiv

An interesting additional thing to know about companies like Enterprise, where you see "LP" in the company name, is that "LP" stands for "Limited Partnership." Not all companies in the midstream energy space are organized under this structure, but many are.

Limited partnership companies enjoy a tax structure that allows the majority of their returns to shareholders to be considered a "return of capital"; while the investor sees a regular cash payment deposited into their investment portfolio, this is not technically a dividend and, as such, is tax deferred. From an accounting perspective, the distributions from limited partnerships reduce the cost basis, which means that investors, more or less, do not pay taxes on the distributions as they are received, but rather when they go to sell the stock—they essentially true-up with the IRS by paying taxes on a large capital gain. Historically, investors in original MLPs would claim that they intended to hold the position until they died and then pass it on to their heirs so that the cost basis could step up to the date-of-death value and avoid more taxes.

The downside to the limited partnership structure is that each year, shareholders receive a statement of their income on a Form K-1, which adds one more set of paperwork to the annual accounting process. Many people and accountants have a bias against this extra step and try to avoid K-1s. Others, however, see it as a small price to pay for tax-deferred income.

Oftentimes, the knowledge that there will be a nasty tax bill waiting for you if you sell the shares helps to encourage sound investor behavior by keeping people invested during market meltdowns when they feel like panicking and cashing out entirely. Between the fear of a tax bill and reliance on a dependable income stream, investments in companies like Enterprise promote solid long-term investment returns by promoting better behavior.

15
THE SHERRIS

"No one spends other people's money as carefully as they spend their own."

—*Milton Friedman*

IN 2011, a colleague of mine had a close friend pass away. Both my colleague and his friend, Edmund, were professional investors and had a decades-long relationship of working together. In their retirement, they chatted daily about stock ideas, the market and geopolitics.

Ideally, my colleague would have taken over the management of his friend's portfolio, which was the sole source of income for the family. However, he was jarred by his friend's sudden heart failure and realized that this could happen to him too, so I was asked to manage the portfolio. Now, enter friend #3, Marcus. Marcus too was shocked by Edmund's death and Marcus too was a professional investor, managing his family's portfolio—and sole source of income.

As I took over management of the portfolio for Edmund's wife, Sherri, friend #3 Marcus thought that bringing in someone else to manage some of their money and serve as a connection point for his wife—coincidentally also named Sherri—would be a prudent idea. Both Sherris, while extremely successful professionals in their own right, were not investors and frankly had little interest in the investment process.

This was Marcus's plan: hire a younger person, preferably a female whom his wife would best relate to, to manage a $1 million portfolio for Sherri. Initially, the portfolio was expected to generate about $50,000 per year of income. Sherri would receive $12,500 per quarter that would be used for travel and life expenses. Marcus hoped that the portfolio's ability to deliver regular income would spark a genuine interest in the family's investments for Sherri. Additionally, Marcus hoped that Sherri would develop a relationship with me so that if anything ever happened to him, she would not be left high and dry without knowing who to turn to or needing to attempt to establish a new, trusting relationship at a time of maximum tragedy and sorrow.

Tragically, Sherri predeceased Marcus in 2021. Upon reflection, Marcus and I realized that the plan was a mix of incredible success and abject failure. Every quarter, I would send Sherri a very thoughtful review of the portfolio with handwritten notes and highlights. I am fairly certain those went straight into the filing cabinet. Over the years, Sherri and I would schedule regular lunch or dinner meetings where,

15: THE SHERRIS

no matter how hard I tried to shoehorn it in, approximately zero investment conversation would take place and I could tell that she would rather be doing, well, just about anything else. Thankfully, over time, a friendship emerged and the conversation, while not investment related, became very enjoyable.

The abject failure part of the experiment was that Sherri never found investing anything but painfully boring. At the root of the problem was that she did not find money or material items very compelling—money was just a means to an end for procuring life's essentials and nothing more. She had everything she wanted: excellent relationships with her husband, children, grandkids and friends. Money was literally just money.

Perhaps counterintuitively, because of Sherri's utter lack of interest in the investment portfolio, her investment behavior was SUPERB! She didn't care if the market was at a peak and never called in a panic asking if we should sell because the S&P 500 was trading at 22x. Similarly, even during the pandemic when the market was down over 30%, she was totally Zen and never called asking if she should sell out because the portfolio was down 30% and the world was clearly about to end. Her income continued to flow into her checking account quarterly and, frankly, she didn't even use all of it up. She lived well within her family's means and enjoyed a wonderful quality of life.

Ten years later, shortly before Sherri passed away, the portfolio that had started at the beginning of 2011 with $1 million and generated $50,000 of income was worth $1.4 million and was generating $77,000. And don't forget, she took out $12,500 every quarter, or $50,000 per year, for a total of $500,000 worth of withdrawals over ten years. Even with that, the account grew! And the dividend income grew!

There is a great behavioral economist at University of California, Los Angeles named Shlomo Benartzi. During the worst times of the pandemic, I heard him give an excellent speech where he essentially advocated for only checking your portfolio statement once a year. He acknowledged the realistic impracticalities of this suggestion, but emphasized that the best investment returns come from long-term patience. One way to encourage that is simply not to look at your account values too often. In the short term, the market is manic and account value fluctuations can unnerve the stoniest of us all. An easy way to contend with that is to avoid checking them too regularly.

As it turns out, Sherri's disinterest and corresponding excellent investment outcome are not unusual. By and large, the clients who care the least seem to enjoy some of the best long-term returns. The opposite is also true: many of the clients who watch every position on a daily—or hourly—basis are jumpy, interfere with the portfolio positions and alter the investment strategies too often, which means they

15: THE SHERRIS

experience worse long-term returns. This makes quarterly reporting fairly miserable because advisors often find themselves delivering excellent returns to the people who care the least and more mediocre returns to clients who care the most.

16

ADVANCE AUTO PARTS

> "Value investing is at its core the marriage of a contrarian streak and a calculator."
>
> —*Seth Klarman*

ONE of the worst investments that I have ever made was in AAP. Losing money was bad enough, but what qualified it as a truly horrible decision was the number of red flags that I excused throughout the research process.

In late 2022, as the stock market sank more deeply into bear market territory, AAP first appeared on my weekly research screen. Notably, its two main competitors—O'Reilly Automotive and Autozone—were not on the weekly screen. After an extensive research process and significant deliberation, at the very end of 2022, I decided to buy shares in AAP and shared the following explanation with clients:

> As many of you know, each week, we run a screen that shows us all of the publicly traded companies in the US with a dividend yield of over 3.5% and a market capitalization of over $150 million. Running a screen ensures that we

remain unbiased with respect to the companies that we are considering for investment and forces us to recognize where and when opportunities are actually being created. A couple of months ago, Advance Auto Parts crept onto the screen and we began a research process to see if it was worth taking a deep dive. What we uncovered was a very compelling opportunity—one that was created by the market throwing many of the proverbial babies out with the bathwater.

Historically, Advance Auto Parts was not a big dividend payer and was thus not a stock that we followed closely. In 2021, however, the company adjusted its capital allocation program to focus more intently on shareholder return and we began to take notice. Historically, AAP's significant cash flow generation was used to acquire, acquire, acquire; but after years of struggling with merger integrations that were messy and elongated, management decided to reap the rewards of the company's remarkably consistent cash flow and begin paying out a significant amount to shareholders in the form of a dividend.

Our research on AAP revealed a company with a consistent history of generating cash flow, even during difficult economic environments. The current management team appears finally to have put the years of messy acquisition integrations behind it and is refocused on managing and growing the company's existing business in a steady and strategic manner, maintaining and hopefully

16: ADVANCE AUTO PARTS

organically growing market share. This investment should be a very slow and steady returner—we will collect the 4.1% annual dividend (which is likely to grow) and expect to enjoy incremental capital appreciation as revenues remain stable, future margins improve as supply chain woes subside and the valuation multiple expands to reflect the improved earnings outlook.

Foolishly, I stepped right into the proverbial value trap by overlooking some serious red flags, which included the following:

- A history of not paying dividends—the dividend was substantial only because of a recent adjustment to the capital allocation program. There was no history of commitment to the dividend; and
- Management's serious lack of execution skill and credibility. At the time of purchase, I knew that O'Reilly and Autozone had far better management teams with long-term track records of superior performance in the auto retailing business, while AAP had always lagged behind. The juicy dividend and discounted valuation clouded my judgment and I overlooked just how inept the management team really was. I thought that they had found religion because they had moved away from the acquisition spree and instituted a dividend. The reality is that bad managers do not magically become good managers.

Dividend investing is ultimately a subset of value investing, and as the wonderful Seth Klarman quote above states, finding good investments is about being a little contrarian and doing some math homework. However, there is so much more to it, because the math works only if the prediction of future cash flows is accurate and, unfortunately, a terrible management team can screw up even the easiest future cash flow generation. Generally, being "a little contrarian" works when applied to how the market is perceiving an industry or fundamentally misunderstanding a business's success prospects. In this case, my contrarian perspective that a management team could "not be that bad" was a colossal failure of judgment.

It just seemed like it could not possibly be that hard to sell auto parts—could it? Clearly, there was not an industry-wide issue, as O'Reilly and Autozone continued to show consistently strong results. It seemed that all AAP had to do was stop making acquisitions and situate its stores in decent locations and it could share in the success of its peers.

As it turned out, I made the wrong call. Shortly after purchasing the stock, I realized a 40% loss and sent the following note to clients:

> As many of you know, six months ago, we added AAP to the Equity Income portfolio. After many years of using their enormous free cash generation to fund acquisitions, the board and management decided to digest the years

16: ADVANCE AUTO PARTS

of acquisitive growth and return the excess cash to shareholders in the form of a hefty dividend. They seemed not only committed to this shareholder return, but extremely capable of executing on the plan. As part of our research process, we looked back to 2007 through 2010 to see how AAP's earnings and revenues held up even during a deep, prolonged recession. We then applied that experience to their current financials and concluded that there was a tremendous margin of safety between current earnings expectations and a worst-case scenario. Well, much to our disappointment, on Wednesday, when they announced their quarterly earnings, management exceeded our very worst expectations by not only completely missing all targets, but also lowering the annual dividend from $6/share to $1/share. Essentially, management decided to abandon its dividend-focused business plan after only two years and the share price was severely punished immediately.

Over the past 24 hours, we have assessed the future upside and have concluded that, while we think the shares are oversold, there is no likely near-term catalyst that would cause the market to reassess AAP. The company's management has made itself radioactive to the dividend-seeking investor base, and growth investors have certainly not forgotten its decade-long inability to use the company's cash flow to drive earnings growth. As such, we do not want to wait around in the hope that the share price recovery will happen quickly. Instead, we have sold our position in AAP and replaced it with a new investment.

Now, it is hard enough to maintain confidence when you manage your own money and have big, dumb losses like this one; but when you are managing other people's money and need to tell them you made a really big mistake, it becomes much harder. In my case, it is compounded by being on CNBC once a week, where I also need to explain to hundreds of thousands of viewers exactly how and why I screwed up.

Maintaining confidence so that you can move forward despite huge mistakes is one of the most important attributes of a successful portfolio manager. In these situations, my wonderful partner, Greg Stanek, always offers the best advice, reminding me: "You know what we do now? We follow the process." This advice is offered during average market corrections, terrifying bear market drops and each and every individual buy or sell decision. The best part of it is that it is the correct advice every time.

17
HENRY VERSUS MARYANNE

"Investing isn't about beating others at their game. It's about controlling yourself at your own game."

—*Ben Graham*

HENRY and MaryAnne are two clients who have never met. They both started with Gilman Hill within a month of each other at the very end of 2018. Both are retired; both enjoy comfortable lives and live well within their means. However, from a temperament perspective, the two are completely different.

Henry is a former corporate tax accountant who watches the news continuously. He participates in a lot of direct private investment deals and, before handing the reins over to us, managed his entire investment portfolio himself. Naturally, the decision to relinquish direct control was extremely difficult and took extensive rounds of conversation, deliberation and consideration. Like most of my clients, Henry both needed and wanted his portfolio to generate income. For years, he had been self-managing his and his wife's portfolios with an eye toward income generation.

By contrast, MaryAnne received a lump sum from her deceased husband's insurance. She had never managed her own money before and had no professional experience in the investment industry. She was referred to me by an acquaintance who basically just told her, "The portfolio they manage will create income for you to live off and they will treat you well." After a brief interview process, she handed the reins over to me.

In 2019, their first full year with me, we had a pretty good run. Returns were positive and both were able to start to build trusting relationships with me. (It simply takes a lot of time to establish a truly confident and comfortable relationship with the person or team to whom you have entrusted your life savings.)

But then, not even a year and a half later, the world spiraled into the Covid-19 pandemic and the stock market tanked, taking everything—including what had been perceived to be "safe" dividend stocks—with it. At the worst, the stock market was down well over 30%. It was hard to say what was scarier for my clients: seeing their life savings plunge by over 30% in a matter of weeks or being completely isolated from friends and family, with the intense fear of catching the virus and ending up intubated on a respirator.

During that time, I channeled my training and experience and communicated, communicated, communicated with my clients. At one point, when I couldn't keep up with calling

17: HENRY VERSUS MARYANNE

each client individually each week, I started doing weekly conference calls. As things settled down a little, they became biweekly; and eventually monthly and then quarterly. At first, though, I knew that the most helpful thing I could do would be to pass on my confidence in the portfolio companies' ability to survive and thrive to my clients. So, week after week, I openly and honestly relayed the conversations that I was having with the management teams of the portfolio investments and how I was thinking and positioning the portfolios to help us get from one side of the pandemic and market plunge to the other—no matter how long that took.

It was not only the communications that brought my clients tremendous emotional comfort; so too did the steady continuation of dividend income that flowed into their portfolios. Even at the worst of the pandemic, most of the companies in which they were invested saw little change to the cash flow generation of their businesses and continued to pay out dividends exactly as they had always planned to. A few companies cut or paused dividends, but that was understandable given the circumstances and they were easily replaceable so that the overall portfolio income ultimately remained intact.

Unfortunately, all the comfort that I was able to bring was not enough for just two of my clients. One of them was Henry, the accountant, who went to cash but stayed as a client. (The other client sold out of everything, pulled his funds out and—as was recently confirmed by his wife, who remained both invested and a client—is still, four years later, sitting on the cash.) Henry simply could not take the anxiety of seeing his portfolio plunge and demanded that I sell everything. I have handwritten notes from this conversation, where I told him that the one thing I knew for certain was that he was making a serious mistake, which would prove extremely costly. He replied, "I know. SELL!" By April, the stock markets had started to recover significantly. By August, the stock market was back to breakeven and ultimately, the S&P 500 turned in a return of 18% for the year. During that time, Henry instructed me to get back into stocks, then back out again, then partially back in again. At some point, I added some bonds and some preferred stocks too. He was simply too uncomfortable to reinvest in the full stock portfolio and instead picked off individual positions. (A mortal sin, in my opinion, is to cherry-pick positions that you think will be the biggest winners. It is always better to own the whole portfolio, as one never really knows which stocks will lead and when it will happen.) For my part, I was loath to aid his terrible investment discipline and decision making, but I knew that it was that or cash—so I did what I could to encourage him to reinvest as much as possible.

Compounding Henry's intense anxiety was the 2020 presidential election. Watching far too much TV news—whose main objective is to catch your eyeballs so they can

17: HENRY VERSUS MARYANNE

collect precious advertising dollars—he was convinced that we were teetering on the brink of a state of martial law and that the city streets would soon be patrolled by tanks.

MaryAnne, on the other hand, focused on her garden and left me alone to manage her portfolio as I saw fit within the context of the guidelines and objectives that we had discussed. In my check-ins with her, she essentially said: "I know that you're doing the best you can and life always seems to go on. Just do what you think is right." There was no drama, no conspiracy theories, no panic attacks (at least none that I, as her money manager, was aware of). MaryAnne allowed the portfolio to be managed with zero emotional input or interference.

Fast forward to today and the inception-to-date compound annualized time-weighted returns of these two clients are vastly different. Henry has only recently broken even and has had an annualized return of just over 1%. This means that, on average, since late 2018, his portfolio has grown by about 1%.

MaryAnne, on the other hand, has a compound annualized return of just below 8%. The total return difference—the wealth creation differential between compounding at 1% and compounding at 8%—is life altering and game changing. At a 1% growth rate, it would take nearly 72 years for a portfolio to double in value. At 8%, it would take just nine years.

MaryAnne's return has more than offset the money that she withdraws to support her retirement. Henry's withdrawals have cut straight into the principal of his portfolio and deteriorated its value.

And why the dramatic difference? Because of their behavior. One person exhibited perfect investment behavior and just gritted her teeth, bore the stress and got through it. The other panicked and cashed out. On winning elections, James Carville famously said, "It's the economy, stupid." On managing a winning investment portfolio, one could say, "It's the behavior, stupid."

At the end of the day—or at the end of the investment portfolio lifespan, which for most investors is many decades long—the winning ticket is good behavior. Whatever strategy it takes for an investor to employ excellent behavior at the worst of times is the investment strategy they should use. For some people, this will be exchange traded funds (ETFs) or mutual funds, where the anxiety of each individual stock move is hidden from their view. For others, individual stock portfolios, where they can see exactly what they own, feel better. Some investors love to see dividend income flowing in, while others do not need or want it and only want to see long-term capital appreciation in their accounts.

If one presumes that over the very long term—which is the many decades of an investor's life and their investment portfolio's life—most strategies will offer the historical

17: HENRY VERSUS MARYANNE

average of an 8%–10% return, then it really does not matter if you are a growth, value, dividend, fund or individual stock investor. All that matters is that you never, ever, EVER, EVER, EVER behave as poorly as Henry did during the worst of 2020. The wealth destruction that he created by selling at the bottom and not getting back in (because, news flash: NO ONE ever gets back in at the right time after they've panic-sold out) destroyed more wealth than could be regained in any reasonable timeframe.

18

SHORT TALES OF MANY WOES AND VALUE TRAPS—NEW YORK COMMUNITY BANK, LUMEN AND CHEROKEE

> "Value traps are cheap for a reason—perhaps an inept and entrenched management, a poor history of capital allocation, or assets whose value is in inexorable decline."
>
> —*Seth Klarman*

ONE of the biggest challenges in dividend investing is avoiding value traps: companies that look like they have a hefty and sustainable dividend and a stable business to support shareholder payouts, but which in reality have entered a period of decline whereby the depreciation in share price will more than offset any return from the dividend income.

As I explained in Chapter 3, it is not the high-growth companies that typically have rich dividend yields, but rather the mature cash cows awash in capital but limited opportunities to reinvest it back into the business to drive future growth. Often, as a company enters real business decline, it can still produce significant cash flows and, if it has a history of dividend payments, can still maintain those. Meanwhile, shrewd investors recognize the inherent decline in the business and start to sell their shares. As the share price drops and the dividend remains intact, the dividend yield can become extremely attractive. Sometimes, when the shrewd investors that incorrectly sold out turn out to be wrong, there is a significant opportunity for dividend investors to step in and lock in a juicy yield on a misunderstood company. Other times, when the shrewd investors are correct, buying at a juicy yield reveals, in retrospect, that you have stepped straight into a value trap—something that any honest value investor has done far more frequently than they would care to admit.

The opening line to Leo Tolstoy's *Anna Karenina* is: "All happy families are alike; each unhappy family is unhappy in its own way." The same is true of stock investments. Each successful investment is about the same—earnings grow and the valuation improves. Each miss, each value trap, is slightly different. Over the years, I have stepped into more than a couple; and despite learning from mistakes and trying not to repeat the same errors in judgment, because each mistake is unhappy in its own way, it is impossible to avoid them forever.

NEW YORK COMMUNITY BANK

One recent miss was New York Community Bank (NYCB). This investment was initiated in 2021, predicated on the thesis that because of its New York City real estate exposure, it was trading at a deep discount to other regional banking peers. Historically, the management team had been considered mediocre but sufficient. A new CEO had recently taken over and, although on the younger side for bank CEOs (late 40s), he was generally viewed as more than capable of running the bank. Then, in 2023, as a micro-US banking crisis erupted, NYCB was able to step in and heroically absorb a failing competitor. For a brief moment, NYCB looked like a shining star and a darling of the regulators; the share price increased and investors like us thought that we were really smart for seeing value in the NYCB shares while others had just seen a mediocre business with a lackluster, inexperienced management team. However, within one short year, the management's inability to successfully navigate the acquisition was laid bare and the bank narrowly avoided liquidation. As it turned out, back in 2021 the shares had traded at a steep discount to peers for a reason: NYCB really was simply a worse company with a weak management team.

LUMEN TECHNOLOGIES

Lumen Technologies was one of my biggest doozies ever and one that I held onto for far too long—from 2017 until 2022. Lumen, which can trace its corporate roots back to the 1930s, became what it is today in the early and mid-2000s through a series of mergers and acquisitions that ultimately resulted in its ownership of over 500,000 miles of fiber assets and mountains of debt. While I fully understood that the world was increasingly going wireless, I also understood that not everything actually happened in the cloud—that ultimately data moved over fiber, the use of which generated billions of dollars in revenues for Lumen. Valuing the company seemed fairly straightforward, as it regularly sold off assets to private and foreign investors at favorable valuations. What I failed to properly account for was the true difficulty of digging out from the debt burden. In my nearly five years of ownership, I collected plenty of dividend income as management continued to pay the dividend, knowing that if they cut it, they would lose almost their entire shareholder base; but I also endured dramatic share price declines as debt restructuring upon debt restructuring failed to find terms favorable enough to truly reduce the debt burden. As it turned out, a broken balance sheet really was insurmountable and in 2022 I finally exited the shares at a steep loss.

CHEROKEE

Cherokee was an iconic kids' clothing brand from my childhood that by 2007, when I started researching the company, was selling exclusively through Target. The clothing was genuinely good quality, soft and well styled. The dividend yield was hefty and the company had a long history of stable dividend payments. As part of the research process, I met with management at Target's headquarters in

18: SHORT TALES OF MANY WOES AND VALUE TRAPS

Minnesota, where both parties seemed committed to a long-term partnership. However, the world was moving toward private labels and Target was slowly but steadily building up its own Cat & Jack brand—which was also good quality, soft and well styled. The writing was on the wall: despite claims to the contrary, Cherokee was a dying business. It had tied its fortunes to Target and had no other source or distribution. As long as the Target contract was in place, Cherokee generated plenty of income, which it diligently paid out to shareholders, keeping the dividend high and the dividend yield even higher as the share price sank to new lows. For non-investors taking a fresh look at Cherokee, they saw a business that had not developed a lifeline for when Target inevitably let its contracts expire. For those of us who stepped on the value trap, we saw hope for contract renewals where none existed. As it turned out, selling clothing brands through the Targets and Walmarts of the world—which were clearly moving toward higher-profitability private labels—was simply a business in decline.

★★★

The beauty of investing is that it is an endless process of discovery. With each mistake made, with each value trap stepped on and even despite each mistake being unique in itself, learning continues and the future promises fewer such mistakes. With fewer mistakes come better returns—and thus, the beauty of compounding again reveals itself: not only do compounded returns generate long-term wealth, but compounded knowledge improves long-term returns!

This is why I share stories of my worst mistakes with you (although please know that this is by no means an exclusive list): I find that many high-profile investors—the ones that everyone listens to—only admit to or discuss their winners, when really it is the losers that generate the greatest opportunities for learning and improvement. If you make one fewer mistake because I shared mine with you and that keeps you from losing, say, 3% of your portfolio through a bum investment, and that saved 3% can now compound at a growth rate of, say, 7%—well, then, the cost of this book, in both money and time, will have been well worth it!

19
DOCTOR KEMP

"Markets can stay irrational longer than you can stay solvent."

—*Joseph Maynard Keynes*

Or my personal—and, if I do say so myself, improved—version:

"Markets can stay irrational longer than you can stay sane!"
—*Jenny Van Leeuwen Harrington*

ONE of the most educational client experiences that I ever had was with a retired cardiologist named Dr. Kemp. When I worked with him in about 2002, he was long since retired and well into his 80s, and he called to talk about his portfolio EVERY. SINGLE. DAY. (Or at least, that's how I remember it and what it felt like.)

Dr. Kemp was a brilliant man. He was a voracious reader of deep, dense historical fiction and non-fiction and loved to tell me what he was reading. He was also a Holocaust survivor who had somehow avoided the concentration camps, but witnessed and experienced horrible atrocities as a young boy growing up in Austria. I remember one story in particular of him witnessing his father being beaten by the SS. This was not a light and fluffy kind of individual, and while the conversation was always interesting, it was never cavalier or superficial.

As the low man on the totem pole, the daily conversation with Dr. Kemp fell to me—and frankly I was delighted to oblige. Back then, my job wasn't that intense and I enjoyed the intellectual rigor and education of our conversations. I even read an extremely long biography of Queen Elizabeth I at his suggestion. Another of his suggestions, *Artemesia*, still sits untouched on my bookshelf years later. One day I'll get to it, but it's just so long and dry looking…

Every day, Dr. Kemp would call and if 33 of the 35 stocks in his portfolio were up, he only cared about the two that were down. It was usually the same few that were down, too. Mind you, this was in the early 2000s, when a 3% move was jarring and over- and underperformance by stocks and sectors were still considered dramatic, even in the low single digits. So a stock could be down 2% and Dr. Kemp would find himself distressed.

Day after day, month after month, year after year, we would talk and talk about the few stocks that were down. Occasionally, I would try to redirect and say, "Oh, but did you see how well such and such is doing?" He would tell me,

19: DOCTOR KEMP

"Yes, and I don't care about that." After years of this, he let slip an interesting insight when he blurted out in frustration, "It's so unfair! You can be wrong over and over and it still ends up okay! If I was wrong once, someone died or I would get sued!"

Today, that statement remains embedded in my consciousness. Some personalities and some jobs require absolute perfection and complete knowledge. I often think that's truest for doctors and structural engineers. If they're off by a millimeter, things can go very, very wrong.

Working with Dr. Kemp was an extraordinary privilege. He treated me with respect and took me seriously at a time when it felt like I was just about the only one who took myself seriously. And I took him seriously too. I didn't see him as a fading old man with some irrational paranoia and a skew toward repetition. I saw him as an extraordinary human who had survived the Nazis; emigrated from Austria, where his family had been forsaken; started afresh in the United States to become a successful cardiologist; built a successful marriage; raised a family; and amassed a nearly $10 million portfolio that was actively used to make his entire family's life easier by helping out with housing, medical and school expenses. Somehow, in addition to all of that, he found the time to read and have meaningful conversations with me—a 20-something nobody, who clearly worked very hard, cared a lot and desperately wanted to become smarter.

Something about Dr. Kemp, above all others, awakened me to the privilege and seriousness of my role as a money manager. Through his eyes, I came to understand that managing money is not a game; it is a profession with tremendous responsibility. The comfort and happiness of families' entire futures rest on our shoulders. To many money managers, generating market-beating performance is a game and their clients' portfolios are merely the vehicle through which they can cobble together the price of entry to play. But to other money managers who know whose money they are actually managing, who genuinely know the people and families who rely on them, portfolio management is a pragmatic endeavor that requires stringent ethics, perpetual education and immense effort; and that must be treated with the utmost sobriety, seriousness and gratitude.

CONCLUDING THOUGHTS

"The individual investor should act consistently as an investor and not as a speculator."

—Ben Graham

As you march forward in the world of dividend income investing, here is a short checklist to keep in mind:

- Always remember the words of Rick at the worst of the Great Financial Crisis in 2009: "Well, if my income is safe, then I'm fine. Don't worry about me. I'm fine!"
- Conducting a thorough and consistent research process is critical to constructing a portfolio of stocks that can generate a dependable and consistent income stream. In this process, above all else, look for a company's philosophical commitment to rewarding shareholders in the form of dividends and for its financial ability to cover the dividend payments going forward.
- Paramount to long-term investment success is being

confident in and comfortable with your unique investment strategy. Confident and comfortable investors are more likely to get through difficult markets with their wits and investments intact. As you contemplate dividend income investing for yourself, think about if this is the right strategy for you. Some people prefer income and some people prefer growth. Different strokes for different folks is okay!

- Be very, very skeptical. If a dividend looks too good to be true, dig extra deep to figure out why. If you are looking at funds, be extremely wary of fees and leverage. Relentlessly unpeel the layers until you discover exactly what lies at the heart of the matter.
- Do not be fearful and try to avoid bear markets or recessions. You will not get the timing right, so focus on managing your portfolio *through* a bear market, not *to* a bear market! Instead, recognize that downturns are natural parts of the investment cycle and view them as incredible opportunities for significant long-term wealth creation. All you need to do is keep your wits about you, do not sell out at the bottom, and when you see the proverbial "blood in the streets," be smart and, if you have cash, buy stocks!

I hope that you love, or have learned to love, dividend investing as much as I do. Through decades of managing a dividend income strategy, I have witnessed firsthand how it

CONCLUDING THOUGHTS

can generate tremendous wealth creation, encourage excellent investment discipline, provide tremendous emotional comfort and, perhaps best of all, create a dependable stream of income to help navigate through all market environments.

EPILOGUE

Over my decades of managing a dividend income strategy, it has surprised me to learn who has needed dividend income to support their lifestyle or simply who has wanted income to add an element of dependable return to their investment portfolios.

Initially, I believed the stereotype that dividend investing was the investment arena for retired people and/or those preparing to retire. In practice, I have found the range of investors interested in income investing to be dramatically broader.

Currently, we manage dividend income strategies for several clients in their twenties and thirties—some are students and some are high caliber professionals with low-paying careers in the arts or education. All have inherited a bit of money and are using it to create a reliable supplemental income to get them through this time of life without needing to directly rely on their parents or take out loans. In Morgan Housel's excellent book, *The Psychology of Money*, he advocates for gifting money to people in their thirties and forties—when it can really help with a home, childcare or education. I think that his suggested timing is exactly right. I have seen firsthand what an extraordinary gift it is to have a bit of a *pressure release valve* for young(ish) people who are working very hard, but not quite making ends meet.

The implementation of a dividend income strategy in these situations can be extremely helpful. Not only does it take off the financial pinch and decrease stress, but it helps create a well-educated investor. Rather than simply foisting a huge amount of money on a new investor, a portfolio that provides a consistent payout of dividend income helps to educate the recipient about investing in a deep, practical, realistic way. It forces the recipient to slow down, plan, think and ask questions. Investing is a long game and there is no need to rush the education for new investors. It is far better to let them learn slowly and thoroughly, and I have witnessed dividend investing create a pathway to do just that.

I have also been surprised by the number of income investors that I have encountered over the years who are quite far from retirement, but really, really love seeing their investments generate income. These skeptical, cynical investors have a fair amount of distrust in "the market" and are willing to potentially forego participating in some of the highest highs as long as they know that their investments will continue to throw off income even during the lowest lows. Interestingly, these investors are frequently people who are also real estate investors and entrepreneurs—both of whom deeply value cash and subscribe to the mentality that *cash is king*.

Of course, the majority of dividend income investors are indeed retirees who use dividend income as a replacement for their previous wages, allowing them to live the retirement life that they had always imagined. As people near retirement and need to get real about replacing their paychecks, they frequently struggle to decide on the best approach. Should they take all of the dividend income as it pays, or set up a recurring flat amount? Should they take the income monthly, quarterly, or annually? In answer to these questions, I always explain that there is no right way, and it has to be what makes each individual, in all of their unique ways, feel comfortable. It all works, and after all, what is the point of having saved money if it cannot bring you comfort?

Lastly, a bit about me. I am 49 years old and have never inherited a penny and, barring a miracle, do not expect to. I also, and this is just my personal preference, want to *age in place*. I like my home and I like puttering about the yard. My goal is to save up enough money that I can, one day, cover the expenses of in-home care if I need it because I do not ever want to burden my kids with that part of life. I used to think that, one day, I'd need someone to drive me around, but by the time I'm there, I expect robotaxis will do the job at a much lower price. With meal delivery services, I'll probably eat pretty well too without needing a cook. In my mind, I'd like to have a portfolio whereby 5% can cover my expenses—and that way, when I have emergencies like needing a new roof or HVAC system, I can dip into the principal if I need to.

I really do not care about beating the market, but I do care deeply about creating a portfolio that will cover my expenses without ever needing to worry about what the market is doing. For me, in all of my unique preferences, this outcome is what I know will make my (very far off in the future) retirement, comfortable.

And once again, the whole point of saving, and having money, is to bring comfort.

A NOTE ON THE COVER

THE cover of this book alludes to a favorite analogy used by my cherished friend, mentor, master asset allocator, brilliant investor, investment committee colleague and all-round superb human being, Charley Ellis.

Years ago, when I first got to know Charley, he compared the experience of having a well-invested, appropriately sized investment portfolio to that of someone sailing on an ocean liner in the middle of the sea versus someone out on the sound for the day in a small fishing boat.

If you were sailing the seas in an ocean liner and were told, "At 5:00 pm, it will be low tide," you would have the wonderful privilege and luxury of saying, "Well, what do I care!" and continue whatever lovely activity you were enjoying. On the other hand, if you were tooling around on a small fishing boat for the day, you would need to check your watch regularly and be extremely careful to be back into the dock well before the tide went out.

An appropriately sized, well-structured investment portfolio is like sailing on an ocean liner, where neither low tide nor a bear market should interrupt whatever you are doing and enjoying.

When I share this analogy, people often ask me what the dollar value is to have their portfolio be an ocean liner and not a small fishing boat. I always answer that this depends entirely on how much they need to spend. For someone that spends $100,000 a year in retirement, a much smaller amount is needed than for someone who spends $500,000. So, unlike in the boating world, in the investing world, almost anyone can afford the proverbial ocean liner—just as long as they are willing to pragmatically match their spending with their savings.

I believe that a dividend income-based investment strategy—where the income an investor needs to support their lifestyle just rolls in through high tides and low tides, bull markets and bear markets—makes for a pragmatic and easier way to get one's own ocean liner!

ACKNOWLEDGMENTS

WITHOUT the enormous brain and perpetual encouragement of my husband, John Harrington, neither Gilman Hill nor this book would ever have happened. For that matter, our children wouldn't be here either! John has painstakingly edited my writing for nearly 30 years, starting with my honors thesis in college. He has edited 18 years' worth of quarterly client letters and every client communication in between. Notwithstanding his best efforts, I have a poor grasp of grammar and punctuation. Miraculously—and despite a million heated brawls over word choices—we are happily married, work together and enjoy each other's company. John is an extraordinary partner in life, a man whose moral compass is permanently stuck at true north and the most selfless cheerleader. I am lucky and deeply appreciative.

I also owe a lifetime of thanks to my extraordinary partner, Greg Stanek. Greg has the patience of a saint and the brain of a Mensa. He is an extraordinarily talented and multifaceted investor, a true triple threat: He is an equally superb analyst, portfolio manager and economist. Greg's partnership has elevated me intellectually as well as professionally. Without Greg's investment talent, excellent character and unbreakable good nature, Gilman Hill would never have become such a robust and joyous place to spend my days!

And of course, an enormous thanks to the team at Gilman Hill, Ashley, Beth, Carl, Corinne, Jake and Brigid, without whom this book could not have happened. They cleared my schedule so that I could write, pitched in with graphics and data, and, as they always do, navigated Gilman Hill seamlessly through every sort of market!

All of my profits from this book will be donated to the Council for Economic Education.